Node.js Multi-Verse Apps

Advanced Strategies for Successful Cross-Platform Application Development with Node.js

Phillips Jeremy

Copyright © 2025 Phillips Jeremy

All rights reserved. No part of this book may be reproduced, stored in a retrieval system, or transmitted, in any form or by any means, electronic, mechanical, photocopying, recording, or otherwise, without the prior written permission of the author, except in the case of brief quotations embodied in critical reviews and certain other noncommercial uses permitted by copyright law.

Table of Contents

Preface

Hey there! If you're holding this book, chances are you're as excited about building amazing applications as I am. And if you're like me, you're also keen on doing it efficiently, reaching as many people as possible without rewriting code for every single platform. That's where the magic of cross-platform development with Node.js comes in. This isn't just another tech book; it's a conversation, a sharing of insights, and a practical guide to building applications that truly connect with users, no matter where they are.

Background and Motivation

I've spent countless hours wrestling with the challenges of building applications that work seamlessly across web, mobile, and desktop. There's something incredibly satisfying about writing code once and seeing it flourish in multiple environments. But, let's be honest, it's not always a walk in the park. We run into platform-specific quirks, performance hiccups, and the constant need to stay up-to-date with evolving technologies. I wrote this book because I wanted to share the strategies and techniques I've learned along the way. I wanted to create a resource that cuts through the noise and provides clear, actionable advice that you can put to use immediately.

Purpose and Scope

This book is designed to equip you with the advanced knowledge and skills needed to build robust cross-platform applications using Node.js. We'll go beyond the basics, exploring how to architect your code for maximum reusability, integrate with platform-specific features when necessary, and optimize performance for a smooth user experience. We'll also tackle the practical aspects of building, testing, and deploying your applications, ensuring they're ready for the real world. Think of this as your practical toolkit for turning great ideas into truly universal applications.

Target Audience

This book is for developers who already have a solid grasp of Node.js and are ready to take their skills to the next level. Whether you're a web developer looking to expand into mobile and desktop, or a seasoned Node.js enthusiast eager to master cross-platform strategies, you'll find valuable insights and practical guidance here. If you are comfortable with asynchronous JavaScript, and basic server side node.js, you'll be well positioned to take advantage of the advanced topics covered.

Organization and Structure

We'll start by refreshing your understanding of core Node.js concepts, focusing on how they relate to cross-platform development. Then, we'll move into advanced techniques, exploring framework integrations, native module interactions, and architectural patterns. We'll cover the nuts and bolts of building and deploying your applications, and finally, we'll discuss testing, debugging, and best practices to ensure your projects are both successful and maintainable. We will also touch on emerging trends that will impact the future of cross platform development.

Invitation to Read

I'm genuinely excited to share this knowledge with you. My hope is that this book will empower you to build amazing applications that reach a wider audience and streamline your development process. So, grab a cup of your favorite beverage, get comfortable, and let's start building some incredible cross-platform applications together. I'm confident that you'll find these strategies and practical tips both useful and inspiring. Let's make some magic happen!

Chapter 1: Introduction to Cross-Platform Development

Hey everyone, welcome! Let's kick things off by talking about something that's become absolutely essential in today's tech scene: cross-platform development. You know, building apps that aren't tied to just one operating system or device. We're going to break down why it's so important, what the different approaches are, and, of course, how Node.js fits into the picture.

1.1 The Need for Cross-Platform Solutions

Alright, let's talk about why we need cross-platform solutions. It's a fundamental question, and understanding the answer will set the stage for everything else we'll cover.

You see, for a long time, building software meant choosing a single platform. If you wanted an app for iPhones, you wrote in Objective-C or Swift. If you wanted it for Android, it was Java or Kotlin. If you needed a desktop application, you were looking at C++, C#, or maybe Python. And if it was a website, then you were dealing with HTML, CSS, and JavaScript.

Now, that's fine if you're only targeting a single platform. But what if you want to reach everyone? What if your idea is so good that you know people using all sorts of devices will want it? That's when the problems start.

Think about it. Each platform has its own language, its own set of tools, its own way of doing things. That means you need to write the same application multiple times, once for each platform. That's a lot of work! Not only do you need to hire developers with different skill sets, but you also need to maintain multiple codebases. If you find a bug, you need to fix it in every version of the app. If you want to add a new feature, you have to implement it multiple times.

And it's not just about the development effort. Think about the time it takes to get your app to market. If you have to build it separately for each platform, you're looking at a much longer development cycle. You might miss out on crucial opportunities or lose ground to competitors who are faster to market.

Then there's the user experience. People expect a consistent experience, no matter what device they're using. If your app looks and feels completely different on iOS and Android, it can be confusing and frustrating for users. They might even decide to use a competitor's app instead.

Let's consider a real-world example. Take a messaging app. Think about how many different devices people use to communicate. They might use a smartphone, a tablet, a laptop, or even a smart watch. If that messaging app only works on one platform, it's not going to be very useful. People need to be able to communicate with their friends and family, no matter what device they're using.

That's why cross-platform solutions are so important. They allow developers to build applications that can run on multiple platforms with a single codebase, or at least with significant code reuse. This reduces development time and effort, lowers costs, and improves consistency.

Now, let's look at a simple code example to illustrate this. Imagine we have a basic function that calculates the area of a rectangle. If we were writing native code for each platform, we'd have to write this function multiple times. But with a cross-platform approach, we can write it once and use it everywhere.

`JavaScript`

```javascript
// JavaScript function to calculate the area of a
rectangle

function calculateRectangleArea(width, height) {

  return width * height;

}
```

```javascript
// Example usage

const area = calculateRectangleArea(5, 10);

console.log("Area:", area);
```

This simple function can be used in a web application, a mobile app built with React Native, or a desktop app built with Electron. That's the power of cross-platform development.

To make it more real, let's consider a slightly more involved example. Imagine we want to fetch data from an API and display it in our app. We can use the fetch API, which is available in most modern browsers and Node.js environments.

JavaScript

```javascript
// Function to fetch data from an API

async function fetchData(url) {

  try {

    const response = await fetch(url);

    if (!response.ok) {
```

```
      throw new Error(`HTTP error! status:
${response.status}`);

   }

   const data = await response.json();

   return data;

 } catch (error) {

   console.error("Error fetching data:", error);

   return null;

 }

}


// Example usage
async function displayData() {

  const data = await
fetchData("https://jsonplaceholder.typicode.com/p
osts/1");

 if (data) {

   console.log("Data:", data);

   // Display data in your app's UI

 }

}
```

```
displayData();
```

This function can be used across web, mobile, and desktop platforms. We write it once, and it works everywhere. That's the advantage we are aiming for.

As a practical exercise, try adapting this example to fetch data from a different API and display it in a simple HTML page or a Node.js console application. This will help solidify your understanding of how cross-platform code can be reused.

The need for cross-platform solutions stems from the desire to reach a wider audience, reduce development costs, and provide a consistent user experience. By using tools and techniques that allow for code reuse, we can build applications that work across multiple platforms without sacrificing quality or efficiency.

1.2 Understanding Cross-Platform Approaches

Okay, so we've established why cross-platform development is important. Now, let's talk about how it actually works. It's not a single, monolithic technique; there are several distinct approaches, each with its own advantages and disadvantages. This is crucial to grasp, because the 'right' approach depends heavily on your specific project goals.

First, let's discuss web-based approaches. This is where you essentially build your application using standard web technologies: HTML, CSS, and JavaScript. You might be thinking, "Wait, that's just a website!" And you're partially right. In this approach, your application runs inside a web browser or a WebView. A WebView is essentially a browser component embedded within a native application.

Think of it this way: you're building a website, but instead of just viewing it in a browser, you're packaging it up as an app. This has some significant benefits. For one, you get incredible code reuse. You write your HTML, CSS, and JavaScript once, and it works across various platforms. This makes development very fast and efficient.

Consider a real-world example: a news application. Many news apps are essentially web applications packaged in a WebView. The content is primarily text and images, which are perfectly suited for web technologies. This allows developers to quickly update content and push changes without needing to go through lengthy app store approval processes.

However, there are trade-offs. Web-based approaches can sometimes suffer from performance limitations, especially when dealing with complex animations or graphics. Access to device-specific features, like the camera or accelerometer, can also be restricted or require workarounds.

Here's a simple example of how you might load a web page into a WebView in a mobile app:

```JavaScript

// Example (Conceptual, platform-specific
implementation needed)

// In a React Native app:

import { WebView } from 'react-native-webview';

import React from 'react';


const MyWebApp = () => {
```

```
return (

  <WebView

    source={{ uri: 'https://www.example.com' }}

    style={{ flex: 1 }}

  />

);

};


export default MyWebApp;
```

This snippet loads a web page into a WebView within a React Native app. Similar implementations exist for other frameworks and native development.

Next, we have native-compiled approaches. These frameworks allow you to write code in a single language, often JavaScript, and then compile it into native code for each target platform. This means you get performance that's much closer to that of a purely native application.

React Native is a prime example of a native-compiled framework. You write your app using JavaScript and React, and React Native compiles it into native components for iOS and Android. This allows you to access device-specific features and achieve excellent performance.

Here's a basic React Native example:

```
JavaScript

// Basic React Native component
```

```
import React from 'react';

import { View, Text, StyleSheet } from
'react-native';


const MyComponent = () => {

  return (

    <View style={styles.container}>

      <Text style={styles.text}>Hello,
Cross-Platform!</Text>

    </View>

  );

};


const styles = StyleSheet.create({

  container: {

    flex: 1,

    justifyContent: 'center',

    alignItems: 'center',

  },

  text: {

    fontSize: 20,
```

```
    },

});
```

```
export default MyComponent;
```

This code is compiled into native UI components for iOS and Android, providing a truly native look and feel.

A real-world example is the Facebook app. Portions of it are built using React Native, allowing Facebook to share code between its iOS and Android versions.

However, native-compiled approaches can be more complex to set up and maintain. You still need to understand platform-specific nuances, and debugging can be more challenging.

Finally, we have hybrid approaches. These try to combine the best of both worlds. You might use web technologies for the core of your app, but then use native code for specific features or performance-critical sections.

Consider a mapping application. The core map display might be built using web technologies, but features like GPS integration or offline map caching might use native code. This allows for rapid development of the core features while still providing access to essential device-specific capabilities.

A practical exercise: try to research a hybrid framework like Capacitor or Cordova. Create a basic app that displays a simple HTML page, then try to add a native plugin that accesses the device's camera. This will give you a hands-on feel for how hybrid approaches work.

In essence, understanding these different cross-platform approaches is essential. Each has its own strengths and weaknesses, and the best choice depends on your project's specific requirements. We'll explore these trade-offs in more detail as we progress.

1.3 Node.js as a Cross-Platform Enabler

Let's discuss how Node.js plays a pivotal role in cross-platform development. You might initially associate Node.js with server-side JavaScript, and that's accurate, but its capabilities extend far beyond backend applications. Node.js, fundamentally, is a runtime environment that allows you to execute JavaScript outside of a web browser. This ability is what makes it so versatile for building cross-platform solutions.

One of the most significant ways Node.js enables cross-platform development is through its capacity to build backend APIs. Think about it: most modern applications, whether web, mobile, or desktop, rely on data from a server. With Node.js, you can create robust, scalable APIs that can serve data to any client, regardless of the platform.

Consider a social media application. The backend that manages user accounts, posts, and interactions can be built using Node.js. This backend API can then be consumed by the web version of the application, the iOS and Android mobile apps, and even a desktop client. This means you write the backend logic once, and it works everywhere.

Here's a basic example of how you might create a simple Node.js API using Express.js:

```
JavaScript

// Example Node.js API with Express.js

const express = require('express');
```

```
const app = express();

const port = 3000;


app.get('/api/posts', (req, res) => {

  const posts = [

    { id: 1, title: 'First Post', content:
'Hello, world!' },

    { id: 2, title: 'Second Post', content:
'Another post.' },

  ];

  res.json(posts);

});


app.listen(port, () => {

  console.log(`Server listening at
http://localhost:${port}`);

});
```

This code creates a simple API endpoint that returns a list of posts. Any application, regardless of the platform, can make a request to this endpoint and receive the data in JSON format.

Another significant area where Node.js shines is in the development of desktop applications using Electron. Electron is a framework that allows you to build cross-platform desktop applications using web technologies: HTML,[1] CSS, and JavaScript. And, crucially, Electron is built on Node.js.

With Electron, you can create applications that run on Windows, macOS, and Linux from a single codebase. This is incredibly powerful. Think of applications like Slack, Discord, and VS Code. They're all built using Electron. This demonstrates the practicality of Node.js in the desktop application space.

Here's a very basic example of a simple Electron application:

JavaScript

```javascript
// main.js (Electron main process)

const { app, BrowserWindow } =
require('electron');


function createWindow() {

  const win = new BrowserWindow({

    width: 800,

    height: 600,

    webPreferences: {

      nodeIntegration: true,

    },

  });
```

```
  win.loadFile('index.html');

}


app.whenReady().then(createWindow);


app.on('window-all-closed', () => {

  if (process.platform !== 'darwin') {

    app.quit();

  }

});


app.on('activate', () => {

  if (BrowserWindow.getAllWindows().length === 0)
{

    createWindow();

  }

});
```

Code snippet

```
<!DOCTYPE html>

<html>
```

```
<head>

   <title>My Electron App</title>

</head>

<body>

   <h1>Hello, Electron!</h1>

   <script>

      console.log('This is running in the Electron
renderer process.');

   </script>

</body>

</html>
```

This code creates a simple window that displays an HTML page. This application can be packaged and distributed for Windows, macOS, and Linux.

While Node.js isn't directly used to build mobile user interfaces, it plays a vital supporting role. Frameworks like React Native, which are used to build mobile apps, often rely on Node.js for development tools, build processes, and backend integrations.

Finally, Node.js is excellent for building command-line tools that work across different operating systems. This is incredibly useful for automating tasks, creating build scripts, and developing developer tools.

Here's a simple example of a Node.js command-line tool:

```
JavaScript
```

```javascript
// my-cli-tool.js

const fs = require('fs');

const filename = process.argv[2];

if (!filename) {

  console.error('Please provide a filename.');

  process.exit(1);

}


fs.readFile(filename, 'utf8', (err, data) => {

  if (err) {

    console.error('Error reading file:', err);

    process.exit(1);

  }

  console.log(data);

});
```

This tool reads the contents of a file and prints it to the console. It works on any operating system that supports Node.js.

As a practical exercise, try creating a simple Node.js command-line tool that takes a filename as an argument and counts the number of lines in the file. This will help you understand how Node.js can be used to build cross-platform tools.

Node.js's versatility and extensive ecosystem make it a powerful tool for cross-platform development. Its ability to build backend APIs, desktop applications, and command-line tools provides developers with the flexibility to create applications that reach a wide audience.

Chapter 2: Node.js Refresher for Cross-Platform

We're going to start with the fundamentals, making sure we're all on the same page. Even if you're a seasoned Node.js developer, it's always good to revisit these concepts, especially when we're thinking about how they apply to cross-platform applications.

2.1 Asynchronous JavaScript and the Event Loop

Let's unpack asynchronous JavaScript and the event loop, because this is the heartbeat of Node.js. It's the reason Node.js can handle so many concurrent operations without getting bogged down, and it's essential for building responsive cross-platform applications.

To understand this, we need to first grasp the concept of synchronous programming. In a synchronous world, tasks execute one after the other, in a linear fashion. If one task takes a long time, everything else waits. Think of it like a single checkout line at a grocery store. Everyone has to wait their turn, even if some people only have a few items.

Now, imagine that grocery store had multiple checkout lines, with some dedicated to express checkout. That's closer to how asynchronous programming works. Node.js is single-threaded, meaning it can only do one thing at a time. However, it's designed to be non-blocking. When it encounters an operation that would normally block the execution, like reading a file or making a network request, it doesn't just sit there and wait. Instead, it delegates that operation to the operating system and registers a callback function.

This is where the event loop comes in. The event loop is a mechanism that continuously monitors the call stack (where functions are executed) and the callback queue (where completed operations are placed). When the call stack is empty, the event loop takes the first callback from the queue and pushes it onto the call stack for execution.[1]

Let's illustrate this with a simple example.

Suppose we want to read a file:

JavaScript

```javascript
const fs = require('fs');


console.log('Start reading file...');


fs.readFile('my-file.txt', 'utf8', (err, data) =>
{

  if (err) {

    console.error('Error reading file:', err);

    return;

  }

  console.log('File content:', data);

});


console.log('This happens after file reading is
initiated.');
```

What happens here? First, "Start reading file..." is printed. Then, fs.readFile is called. This function doesn't block the execution. Instead, it tells the operating system to read the file, and provides a callback function that will be executed when the file is read. The execution continues, and "This happens after file reading is initiated." is printed.

Later, when the file is read, the operating system places the callback function into the callback queue. The event loop then takes this callback and pushes it onto the call stack, which results in "File content: ..." being printed.

To see this in action, create a file named my-file.txt with some text in it and run the code. You'll observe that the messages are printed in the order described above, not in the order the code is written.

Now, let's look at a more practical example: fetching data from an API.

JavaScript

```
async function fetchData(url) {

  try {

    const response = await fetch(url);

    if (!response.ok) {

      throw new Error(`HTTP error! status:
${response.status}`);

    }

    const data = await response.json();

    return data;

  } catch (error) {
```

```
    console.error('Error fetching data:', error);

    return null;

  }

}


async function displayData() {

  const data = await
fetchData('https://jsonplaceholder.typicode.com/p
osts/1');

  if (data) {

    console.log('Data:', data);

  }

}


displayData();

console.log('This happens while data is being
fetched.');
```

Here, fetchData uses async and await to handle the asynchronous operation of fetching data from the API. The await keyword pauses the execution of the displayData function until the fetchData promise resolves. However, it doesn't block the entire Node.js process. The "This happens while data is being fetched." message is printed before the API response is processed.

This is critical in cross-platform development. Imagine building a desktop application with Electron. You want to keep the UI responsive, even when performing long-running tasks like downloading files or processing data. Asynchronous operations allow you to do this.

As a practical exercise, let's create a scenario where we fetch data from multiple APIs concurrently. We'll use Promise.all to wait for all the promises to resolve.

JavaScript

```javascript
async function fetchMultipleData(urls) {

  try {

    const promises = urls.map(url =>
fetch(url).then(response => {

      if (!response.ok) {

        throw new Error(`HTTP error! status:
${response.status}`);

      }

      return response.json();

    }));

    const results = await Promise.all(promises);

    return results;

  } catch (error) {

    console.error('Error fetching data:', error);

    return null;
```

```
    }

}


async function displayMultipleData() {

  const urls = [

'https://jsonplaceholder.typicode.com/posts/1',

'https://jsonplaceholder.typicode.com/todos/1',

  ];

  const data = await fetchMultipleData(urls);

  if (data) {

    console.log('Data:', data);

  }

}


displayMultipleData();

console.log('This happens while data is being
fetched from multiple URLs.');
```

In this example, fetchMultipleData fetches data from two APIs concurrently. The Promise.all function waits for both promises to resolve before returning the results. This allows us to fetch data more efficiently.

Try running this code and observe the output. You'll see that the "This happens while data is being fetched from multiple URLs." message is printed before the API responses are processed.

Understanding asynchronous JavaScript and the event loop is crucial for building responsive and efficient cross-platform applications. It's the foundation upon which Node.js's non-blocking I/O model is built, and it's what makes Node.js so well-suited for handling concurrent operations.

2.2 Module System and Package Management (npm/yarn)

Let's delve into the module system and package management in Node.js. This is another fundamental aspect of Node.js development, and it's especially critical when building cross-platform applications. A well-organized and modular codebase is essential for code reuse and maintainability.

Node.js has a built-in module system that allows you to break your code into smaller, reusable pieces. This is achieved through the require function, which is used to import modules. A module can be a file or a directory containing a package.json file.

Consider a simple example. Let's say you have a utility function that you want to use in multiple parts of your application.

You can create a module for this function:

JavaScript

```
// utils.js

function formatCurrency(amount) {

  return `$${amount.toFixed(2)}`;
```

```javascript
}
```

```javascript
module.exports = {

    formatCurrency,

};
```

And then, you can import this module in another file:

JavaScript

```javascript
// app.js

const utils = require('./utils');


const price = 12.345;

const formattedPrice =
utils.formatCurrency(price);

console.log(formattedPrice);
```

This simple example demonstrates how you can create and import modules. This allows you to keep your code organized and reusable.

Now, let's talk about package management. Node.js has two popular package managers: npm (Node Package Manager) and yarn. These tools allow you to install and manage third-party libraries. This is incredibly useful because you don't have to write everything from scratch.

Consider the Express.js library. Express.js is a popular web framework for Node.js. To use it in your application, you need to install it using npm or yarn.

Here's how you can install Express.js using npm:

Bash

npm install express

And here's how you can install it using yarn:

Bash

yarn add express

Once you've installed Express.js, you can use it in your application:

JavaScript

```javascript
// app.js

const express = require('express');

const app = express();

const port = 3000;


app.get('/', (req, res) => {

  res.send('Hello, World!');

});


app.listen(port, () => {
```

```
  console.log(`Server listening at
http://localhost:${port}`);
```

```
});
```

This example creates a simple web server using Express.js. This demonstrates how you can use third-party libraries to add functionality to your application.

A real-world example of using npm or yarn is when working with a front-end framework like React or Vue. These frameworks have extensive ecosystems of packages that you can install and use in your applications. For example, you might use a library like axios to make HTTP requests or a library like lodash to manipulate arrays.

Here's an example of using axios to fetch data from an API:

JavaScript

```
// app.js
```

```
const axios = require('axios');
```

```
async function fetchData(url) {

  try {

    const response = await axios.get(url);

    return response.data;

  } catch (error) {

    console.error('Error fetching data:', error);
```

```
    return null;

  }

}


async function displayData() {

  const data = await
fetchData('https://jsonplaceholder.typicode.com/p
osts/1');

  if (data) {

    console.log('Data:', data);

  }

}


displayData();
```

To use axios, you need to install it using npm or yarn:

Bash

npm install axios

or

Bash

yarn add axios

This example demonstrates how you can use axios to fetch data from an API.

A practical exercise: create a Node.js application that uses a third-party library, like moment or uuid, to perform a specific task. For example, you could use moment to format dates or uuid to generate unique identifiers.

Understanding the module system and package management is crucial for building scalable and maintainable applications. It allows you to organize your code into reusable components and leverage the vast ecosystem of third-party libraries. This is especially important when building cross-platform applications, where code reuse is essential.

2.3 Building Basic Node.js Servers

Let's talk about building basic Node.js servers. This is a core competency for any Node.js developer, and it's particularly important for cross-platform applications. Node.js's ability to create robust backend APIs makes it a powerful tool for serving data to web, mobile, and desktop clients.

When we talk about building a Node.js server, we're essentially talking about creating an application that listens for incoming HTTP requests and sends back responses. Node.js provides a built-in http module that allows you to create servers. However, for more complex applications, developers often use frameworks like Express.js, which simplifies server creation and provides additional features.

Let's start with a simple example using the http module:

JavaScript

```
const http = require('http');
```

```
const server = http.createServer((req, res) => {
```

```javascript
  res.writeHead(200, { 'Content-Type':
'text/plain' });

  res.end('Hello, World!\n');

});



const port = 3000;



server.listen(port, () => {

  console.log(`Server listening at
http://localhost:${port}`);

});
```

This code creates a server that listens on port 3000. When a client makes a request to this server, it responds with "Hello, World!".

Now, let's explore a more practical example using Express.js. Express.js simplifies the process of creating routes and handling different HTTP methods.

JavaScript

```javascript
const express = require('express');

const app = express();

const port = 3000;



app.get('/', (req, res) => {

  res.send('Hello, Express!');
```

```javascript
});


app.get('/api/posts', (req, res) => {

  const posts = [

    { id: 1, title: 'First Post', content:
'Hello, world!' },

    { id: 2, title: 'Second Post', content:
'Another post.' },

  ];

  res.json(posts);

});


app.listen(port, () => {

  console.log(`Server listening at
http://localhost:${port}`);

});
```

In this example, we've created two routes: / and /api/posts. The / route responds with a simple text message, and the /api/posts route responds with a JSON array of posts.

Express.js makes it easy to handle different HTTP methods, like POST, PUT, and DELETE. For example, let's create a route that handles POST requests:

JavaScript

```javascript
app.post('/api/posts', (req, res) => {

    const newPost = req.body; // Assuming you have
middleware to parse JSON

    // Save the new post to a database or file

    console.log('New post:', newPost);

    res.status(201).json(newPost);

});
```

To handle JSON data in the request body, you need to use middleware like express.json():

JavaScript

app.use(express.json());

This middleware parses incoming JSON requests and makes the data available in req.body.

A real-world example of building a Node.js server is creating a RESTful API for a mobile application. The mobile app can send HTTP requests to the API to retrieve and update data.

Let's consider an example of building an API for a simple to-do list application.

```javascript
JavaScript

const express = require('express');

const app = express();

const port = 3000;
```

```javascript
app.use(express.json());


let todos = [

  { id: 1, text: 'Learn Node.js' },

  { id: 2, text: 'Build an API' },

];


app.get('/api/todos', (req, res) => {

  res.json(todos);

});


app.post('/api/todos', (req, res) => {

  const newTodo = { id: todos.length + 1, text:
req.body.text };

  todos.push(newTodo);

  res.status(201).json(newTodo);

});


app.listen(port, () => {

  console.log(`Server listening at
http://localhost:${port}`);
```

```
});
```

This API provides endpoints to retrieve and create to-do items. The mobile app can use these endpoints to display and manage the to-do list.

As a practical exercise, try creating a Node.js server that serves static files, like HTML, CSS, and JavaScript. This will help you understand how Node.js can be used to build web applications.

```JavaScript
const express = require('express');

const path = require('path');


const app = express();

const port = 3000;


app.use(express.static(path.join(__dirname,
'public')));


app.listen(port, () => {

   console.log(`Server listening at
http://localhost:${port}`);

});
```

Create a public directory in your project and place your static files inside it. This server will serve those files.

Building Node.js servers is a fundamental skill for cross-platform development. It allows you to create robust backend APIs that can be used by various clients. Understanding how to create routes, handle different HTTP methods, and serve static files is essential for building real-world applications.

2.4 Core Node.js Concepts for Cross-Platform Development

Alright, let's focus on the core Node.js concepts that become particularly important when building cross-platform applications. We're not just talking about the basics anymore; we're looking at the tools and techniques that allow us to write efficient, reusable, and maintainable code across different platforms.

First, let's discuss streams. In Node.js, streams are used to handle large amounts of data efficiently. Instead of loading the entire dataset into memory at once, streams allow you to process data in chunks. This is crucial when dealing with files, network requests, or any other I/O operation that involves large amounts of data.

Consider a scenario where you need to read a large file and process its contents. Without streams, you'd have to load the entire file into memory, which could lead to performance issues or even crashes. With streams, you can read the file in chunks and process each chunk as it becomes available.

Here's an example of using streams to read a large file:

```javascript
JavaScript

const fs = require('fs');


const readStream =
fs.createReadStream('large-file.txt', 'utf8');
```

```
readStream.on('data', (chunk) => {

  console.log('Received chunk:', chunk);

  // Process the chunk of data

});



readStream.on('end', () => {

  console.log('Finished reading file.');

});



readStream.on('error', (err) => {

  console.error('Error reading file:', err);

});
```

In this example, fs.createReadStream creates a readable stream that reads the file in chunks. The data event is emitted each time a chunk of data is available, and the end event is emitted when the entire file has been read.

A practical exercise: try creating a Node.js application that uses streams to read a large file and write it to another file, transforming the data in some way. For example, you could convert the data to uppercase or filter out certain lines.

Next, let's talk about buffers. Buffers are used to represent binary data in Node.js. This is crucial when working with images, audio, or other binary files. Buffers allow you to manipulate binary data directly.

Here's an example of reading an image file into a buffer:

```
JavaScript

const fs = require('fs');


fs.readFile('image.jpg', (err, data) => {

  if (err) {

    console.error('Error reading file:', err);

    return;

  }

  // 'data' is a buffer containing the image data

  console.log('Image data:', data);

});
```

In this example, fs.readFile reads the image file and returns a buffer containing the image data. You can then manipulate this buffer using various buffer methods.

A real-world example of using buffers is when building an image processing application. You might use a library like sharp to resize or transform images, and sharp works with buffers to manipulate the image data.

Finally, let's discuss events. The event-driven nature of Node.js is fundamental to its asynchronous programming model.

Understanding how to work with events is essential for building responsive applications.

Node.js has a built-in EventEmitter class that allows you to create and emit custom events. This is useful for building loosely coupled applications where different parts of the application can communicate with each other without knowing about each other.

Here's an example of using the EventEmitter class:

JavaScript

```javascript
const EventEmitter = require('events');



class MyEmitter extends EventEmitter {}



const myEmitter = new MyEmitter();



myEmitter.on('data', (data) => {

  console.log('Received data:', data);

});



myEmitter.emit('data', 'Hello, world!');
```

In this example, we create a custom event emitter and listen for the data event. When the data event is emitted, the callback function is executed.

A practical exercise: create a Node.js application that uses the EventEmitter class to simulate a simple chat application. When a user sends a message, emit an event that other users can listen for.

These core Node.js concepts—streams, buffers, and events—are crucial for building efficient and maintainable cross-platform applications. They allow you to handle large amounts of data, manipulate binary data, and build loosely coupled applications. Mastering these concepts will significantly enhance your ability to build robust cross-platform applications.

Chapter 3: Architecting for Cross-Platform with Node.js

When we build applications for multiple platforms, we need to think about architecture from the start. It's not just about writing code that works; it's about writing code that's maintainable, scalable, and adaptable to different environments.

3.1 Designing Platform-Agnostic APIs

Let's really get into the nitty-gritty of designing platform-agnostic APIs. This is a topic that sits right at the heart of effective cross-platform development. If you get this right, you'll lay a solid foundation for your application, making it adaptable and future-proof.

When we say "platform-agnostic," we mean that the API shouldn't care who's asking for the data. It shouldn't make assumptions about whether the request is coming from a web browser, a mobile app, a desktop client, or even some other system. The API's job is to serve data in a consistent, predictable way, regardless of the client.

The cornerstone of this approach is data serialization. We need a format that's universally understood, and that's where JSON (JavaScript Object Notation) comes in. JSON is lightweight, human-readable, and supported by virtually every programming language and platform. It's the perfect choice for transferring data between your backend and your clients.

Let's illustrate this with a practical example. Imagine we're building a social media application. We need an API endpoint that returns a list of user profiles.

```
JavaScript
```

```javascript
// Example API endpoint for user profiles

app.get('/api/users', (req, res) => {

  const users = [

    { id: 1, username: 'john_doe', fullName:
'John Doe', profilePicture:
'https://example.com/john.jpg' },

    { id: 2, username: 'jane_smith', fullName:
'Jane Smith', profilePicture:
'https://example.com/jane.jpg' },

  ];

  res.json(users);

});
```

This endpoint returns a JSON array of user profiles. Notice how the data is structured in a clear, consistent way. Each user profile has an id, username, fullName, and profilePicture. Any client can parse this JSON data and display it in its user interface.

Now, let's consider a scenario where we need to handle user authentication. We could create an endpoint that accepts a username and password and returns an authentication token.

```javascript
JavaScript

// Example API endpoint for user authentication

app.post('/api/auth', (req, res) => {

  const { username, password } = req.body;

  // Validate username and password
```

```
  if (username === 'john_doe' && password ===
'password123') {

    const token =
'eyJhbGciOiJIUzI1NiIsInR5cCI6IkpXVCJ9...'; //
Generate a JWT

    res.json({ token });

  } else {

    res.status(401).json({ message: 'Invalid
credentials' });

  }

});
```

Here, we're using JSON to send back both success and error responses. This keeps the API consistent and easy to understand.

But it's not just about the data format. We also need to think about API design principles. REST (Representational State Transfer) is a popular architectural style for building web APIs. RESTful APIs are designed around resources and use standard HTTP methods like GET, POST, PUT, and DELETE to perform operations on those resources.

For example, instead of creating separate endpoints for creating, reading, updating, and deleting posts, we can use a single endpoint and different HTTP methods:

- GET /api/posts: Retrieves a list of posts.
- POST /api/posts: Creates a new post.
- PUT /api/posts/:id: Updates an existing post.
- DELETE /api/posts/:id: Deletes a post.

This makes the API more consistent and easier to use.

Versioning is another critical aspect of API design. As your application evolves, you might need to make changes to your API. But you don't want to break existing clients. That's where versioning comes in.

You can version your API by including a version number in the URL:

```javascript
JavaScript

// Example versioned API endpoint

app.get('/api/v1/posts', (req, res) => {

    // ...

});



app.get('/api/v2/posts', (req, res) => {

    // ...

});
```

This allows you to introduce breaking changes in v2 without affecting clients that are using v1.

A practical exercise: design a RESTful API for a simple e-commerce application. Think about the different resources you'll need (e.g., products, orders, users) and the different operations you'll need to support. Also, consider how you would handle authentication and versioning.

A real-world example is the Stripe API. It is well documented, and very consistent. It uses standard HTTP methods, and has well defined error messages, and uses versioning. This makes it easier for developers on any platform to use.

Designing platform-agnostic APIs is about creating a contract between your backend and your clients. By using JSON, following REST principles, and implementing versioning, you can build APIs that are robust, maintainable, and adaptable to different platforms.

3.2 Creating Reusable Node.js Modules

Let's talk about creating reusable Node.js modules. This is a topic that's fundamental to writing clean, maintainable, and scalable code, especially in the context of cross-platform development. When you're building applications that span multiple environments, code reuse isn't just a nice-to-have; it's a necessity.

Node.js has a powerful module system that allows you to organize your code into self-contained, reusable units. This is achieved through the require function, which is used to import modules, and the module.exports object, which is used to export modules.

Think of modules as building blocks. You create individual blocks, each with a specific purpose, and then assemble them to build your application. This approach has several advantages. It promotes code organization, reduces redundancy, and makes it easier to test and maintain your code.

Let's start with a simple example. Suppose we have a set of utility functions that we want to use in multiple parts of our application.

We can create a module for these functions:

```javascript
JavaScript

// string-utils.js

function capitalize(str) {

  if (!str) return '';
```

```javascript
    return str.charAt(0).toUpperCase() +
str.slice(1);

}


function trimWhitespace(str) {

    if (!str) return '';

    return str.trim();

}


function isValidEmail(str) {

    if (!str) return false;

    const emailRegex =
/^[^\s@]+@[^\s@]+\.[^\s@]+$/;

    return emailRegex.test(str);

}


module.exports = {

    capitalize,

    trimWhitespace,

    isValidEmail,

};
```

In this example, we've created a module that exports three utility functions: capitalize, trimWhitespace, and isValidEmail.

We can then import this module in other parts of our application:

JavaScript

```
// app.js

const stringUtils = require('./string-utils');


const capitalizedName =
stringUtils.capitalize('john');

const trimmedString =
stringUtils.trimWhitespace('  hello  ');

const isValid =
stringUtils.isValidEmail('test@example.com');


console.log(capitalizedName, trimmedString,
isValid);
```

This allows us to reuse these functions in multiple parts of our application without duplicating code.

Now, let's consider a more complex example. Imagine we're building a library for making HTTP requests. We might create a module that handles authentication, error handling, and request formatting.

JavaScript

```
// http-client.js
```

```javascript
const axios = require('axios');


async function makeRequest(url, method = 'GET',
data = null, headers = {}) {

  try {

    const response = await axios({

      url,

      method,

      data,

      headers,

    });

    return response.data;

  } catch (error) {

    if (error.response) {

      console.error('HTTP error:',
error.response.status, error.response.data);

      throw error.response.data;

    } else {

      console.error('Network error:',
error.message);

      throw error.message;

    }
```

```
    }

}


async function get(url, headers = {}) {

    return makeRequest(url, 'GET', null, headers);

}


async function post(url, data, headers = {}) {

    return makeRequest(url, 'POST', data, headers);

}


// ... other HTTP methods ...


module.exports = {

    get,

    post,

    // ... other HTTP methods ...

};
```

This module encapsulates the logic for making HTTP requests using the axios library. We can then import this module in other parts of our application and use it to make requests.

A real-world example of creating reusable modules is when building a logging library. You might create a module that handles logging to different destinations, like files or databases. This module can then be used by all parts of your application to log messages.

A practical exercise: create a Node.js module that provides utility functions for working with dates. For example, you could create functions for formatting dates, calculating the difference between two dates, or checking if a date is valid.

JavaScript

```javascript
// date-utils.js

const moment = require('moment');


function formatDate(date, format = 'YYYY-MM-DD') {
    if (!date) return '';

    return moment(date).format(format);
}


function diffInDays(date1, date2) {
    if (!date1 || !date2) return null;

    return moment(date1).diff(moment(date2),
'days');
}
```

```javascript
function isValidDate(date) {

  if (!date) return false;

  return moment(date, moment.ISO_8601,
true).isValid();

}



module.exports = {

  formatDate,

  diffInDays,

  isValidDate,

};
```

Remember, the goal of creating reusable modules is to make your code more organized, maintainable, and reusable. This is especially important when building cross-platform applications, where code reuse is essential.

3.3 Abstraction Layers for Platform Differences

Let's talk about abstraction layers, a critical concept when developing cross-platform applications. When you're building for multiple environments, you'll invariably encounter platform-specific differences. These variations can range from file system interactions to device hardware access, and they can quickly complicate your codebase if not handled properly. That's where abstraction layers come in.

An abstraction layer essentially acts as a mediator. It hides the underlying platform-specific details behind a consistent, unified interface. This allows you to write code that works across different platforms without needing to know the specifics of each one.

Consider a simple example: file system access. On the web, you might use the File API, which is asynchronous and browser-specific. On mobile, you might use native modules or platform-specific file access APIs. On Node.js, you'd use the fs module, which is synchronous or asynchronous.

Without an abstraction layer, you'd have to write different code for each platform. This leads to code duplication and makes your application harder to maintain. With an abstraction layer, you can create a single interface that works across all platforms.

Here's a conceptual example of how you might create an abstraction layer for file system access:

JavaScript

```javascript
// file-system.js

function readFile(filePath, encoding = 'utf8') {

    if (typeof window !== 'undefined' &&
window.FileReader) {

      // Web environment

      return new Promise((resolve, reject) => {

        fetch(filePath)

          .then(response => response.blob())

          .then(blob => {

            const reader = new FileReader();
```

```
        reader.onload = event =>
resolve(event.target.result);

        reader.onerror = reject;

        reader.readAsText(blob, encoding);

    });

  });

} else if (typeof navigator !== 'undefined' &&
navigator.product === 'ReactNative') {

    // React Native environment (requires native
module)

    const RNFS = require('react-native-fs');

    return RNFS.readFile(filePath, encoding);

} else {

    // Node.js environment

    const fs = require('fs');

    return new Promise((resolve, reject) => {

        fs.readFile(filePath, encoding, (err, data)
=> {

        if (err) reject(err);

        else resolve(data);

        });

    });
```

```
    }

}
```

```
module.exports = {

    readFile,

};
```

In this example, the readFile function hides the platform-specific differences behind a common interface. You can use this function to read files regardless of the platform.

A real-world example of using abstraction layers is when building a cross-platform UI framework. The framework might provide a common interface for creating buttons, text inputs, and other UI elements, and then use platform-specific implementations under the hood.

For instance, React Native does this. You write code using React components, and React Native translates those components into native UI elements for iOS and Android.

Let's consider another example: geolocation. The geolocation API is different on different platforms. On the web, you use the navigator.geolocation API. On mobile, you might use native modules.

Here's a conceptual example of how you might create an abstraction layer for geolocation:

```
JavaScript
```

```
// geolocation.js
```

```
function getCurrentPosition() {
```

```javascript
  if (typeof navigator !== 'undefined' &&
navigator.geolocation) {

    // Web environment

    return new Promise((resolve, reject) => {


navigator.geolocation.getCurrentPosition(resolve,
reject);

    });

  } else if (typeof navigator !== 'undefined' &&
navigator.product === 'ReactNative') {

    // React Native environment (requires native
module)

    const Geolocation =
require('react-native-geolocation-service');

    return new Promise((resolve, reject) => {

      Geolocation.getCurrentPosition(resolve,
reject);

    });

  } else {

    // No geolocation available

    return Promise.reject(new Error('Geolocation
not available'));

  }

}
```

```
module.exports = {

  getCurrentPosition,

};
```

In this example, the getCurrentPosition function provides a common interface for getting the device's location.

A practical exercise: create an abstraction layer for accessing the device's camera. The camera API is different on different platforms. Create a module that provides a common interface for taking pictures.

Using abstraction layers is about creating a clean separation between your application logic and the underlying platform-specific details. This allows you to write code that is more portable, maintainable, and testable. It's a key technique for building successful cross-platform applications.

Chapter 4: Framework Integrations

In this chapter, we're going to see how Node.js plays a pivotal role in building applications that work on multiple platforms. We'll get into the specifics of using frameworks that leverage Node.js to create desktop and mobile apps, and we'll also discuss strategies for code sharing.

4.1 Building Desktop Apps with Electron and Node.js

Okay, let's dive into the specifics of building desktop applications with Electron and Node.js. This is a powerful combination that allows you to create cross-platform desktop applications using web technologies. It's a game-changer for developers who are already familiar with HTML, CSS, and JavaScript and want to extend their reach to the desktop environment.

Electron, at its core, is a framework that essentially bundles a Chromium rendering engine (the same one that powers Google Chrome) and a Node.js runtime into a single application. This unique architecture gives you the best of both worlds. You can use web technologies for your application's user interface and Node.js for backend functionalities and system-level interactions.

Think of it this way: your application's window is essentially a web browser, and Node.js is running in the background, providing access to the operating system's resources. This means you can build desktop applications with the same tools and techniques you use for web development, but with the added power of Node.js.

Let's break down the key components and concepts:

The Main Process and the Renderer Process

Electron applications have two types of processes: the main process and the renderer process.

- The Main Process: This is the entry point for your Electron application. It's responsible for creating and managing application windows, handling system events, and interacting with the operating system. The main process runs in a Node.js environment.
- The Renderer Process: This process runs in a separate window and is responsible for rendering the web page. Each window in your Electron application has its own renderer process. The renderer process also runs in a Node.js environment.

It's important to understand the distinction between these two processes because they have different capabilities and communicate with each other in specific ways.

A Basic Electron Application Structure

A typical Electron application has the following structure:

- package.json: This file contains metadata about your application, including dependencies and scripts.
- main.js: This is the entry point for your Electron application and contains the main process code.
- index.html: This file contains the HTML structure of your application's user interface.
- renderer.js (optional): This file contains JavaScript code that runs in the renderer process and interacts with the HTML.
- styles.css (optional): This file contains CSS styles for your application's user interface.

A Simple Electron Application Example

Let's walk through a simple example of creating an Electron application:

1. Create a Project:

Create a new directory for your project and initialize it with npm:

```bash
mkdir my-electron app
cd my-electron-app
npm init -y
```

2. Install Electron:

Install the `electron` package:

```bash
npm install electron
```

3. Create main.js:

Create a file named `main.js` with the following code:

```javascript
const { app, BrowserWindow } =
require('electron');

const path = require('path');


function createWindow() {

  const mainWindow = new BrowserWindow({

    width: 800,

    height: 600,

    webPreferences: {

      nodeIntegration: true,

      contextIsolation: false,

    },

  });



  mainWindow.loadFile(path.join(__dirname,
'index.html'));

}


app.whenReady().then(createWindow);
```

```
app.on('window-all-closed', () => {

  if (process.platform !== 'darwin') {

    app.quit();

  }

});



app.on('activate', () => {

  if (BrowserWindow.getAllWindows().length === 0)
{

    createWindow();

  }

});

```

This code:

Imports the necessary modules from Electron.

Defines a `createWindow` function that creates a new `BrowserWindow` instance.

Loads `index.html` into the window.

Handles application lifecycle events like `ready`, `window-all-closed`, and `activate`.

Important: `nodeIntegration` and `contextIsolation` are set for simplicity in this example. In production, you should handle security implications carefully.

4. Create index.html:

Create a file named `index.html` with the following code:

```html
<!DOCTYPE html>

<html>

<head>

  <title>My Electron App</title>

</head>

<body>

  <h1>Hello, Electron!</h1>

  <script>

    console.log('This is running in the Electron renderer process.');

  </script>

</body>

</html>
```

This is a simple HTML file that will be displayed in the Electron window.

5. Run the Application:

Add a script to your `package.json` file to run the application:

```json
"scripts": {
  "start": "electron ."
}
```

Then, run the application:

```bash
npm start
```

This will launch the Electron application, and you should see a window displaying "Hello, Electron!".

Inter-Process Communication (IPC)

The main process and the renderer process often need to communicate with each other. Electron provides a mechanism for this called Inter-Process Communication (IPC).

- The ipcMain module is used in the main process to receive messages from the renderer process.
- The ipcRenderer module is used in the renderer process to send messages to the main process.

This communication allows you to perform operations that require access to system resources in the main process and then send the results back to the renderer process for display.

Electron and Node.js Capabilities

With Electron, you have access to the full power of Node.js. This means you can:

- Access the file system (fs module).
- Perform network operations (http, https modules).
- Execute system commands (child_process module).
- Use any Node.js module available on npm.

This allows you to build desktop applications with complex functionalities.

A More Practical Example: File System Interaction

Let's extend our example to demonstrate file system interaction:

1. Modify index.html:

Add a button and a display area to `index.html`:

```html
<!DOCTYPE html>

<html>
```

```html
<head>

  <title>My Electron App</title>

</head>

<body>

  <h1>Hello, Electron!</h1>

  <button id="readFileBtn">Read File</button>

  <div id="fileContent"></div>

  <script src="renderer.js"></script>

</body>

</html>
```
```

**2.** Create renderer.js:

**Create a file named `renderer.js` with the following code:**

```javascript
const { ipcRenderer } = require('electron');


const readFileBtn =
document.getElementById('readFileBtn');

const fileContent =
document.getElementById('fileContent');
```
```

```javascript
readFileBtn.addEventListener('click', () => {

  ipcRenderer.send('read-file');

});


ipcRenderer.on('file-read', (event, data) => {

  fileContent.textContent = data;

});
```
```

**This code:**

Gets references to the button and the display area.

 Sends a message to the main process when the button is clicked.

Listens for a message from the main process and displays the file content.

**3.** Modify main.js:

**Modify `main.js` to handle the `read-file` message:**

```javascript
```
```

```javascript
const { app, BrowserWindow, ipcMain, dialog } =
require('electron');

const path = require('path');

const fs = require('fs');


function createWindow() {

  const mainWindow = new BrowserWindow({

    width: 800,

    height: 600,

    webPreferences: {

      nodeIntegration: true,

      contextIsolation: false,

    },

  });


  mainWindow.loadFile(path.join(__dirname,
'index.html'));

}


app.whenReady().then(createWindow);
```

```javascript
app.on('window-all-closed', () => {

  if (process.platform !== 'darwin') {

    app.quit();

  }

});


app.on('activate', () => {

  if (BrowserWindow.getAllWindows().length === 0)
{

    createWindow();

  }

});


ipcMain.on('read-file', (event) => {

  dialog.showOpenDialog({

    properties: ['openFile']

  }).then(result => {

    if (result.filePaths &&
result.filePaths.length > 0) {

      fs.readFile(result.filePaths[0], 'utf8',
(err, data) => {

        if (err) {
```

```
            console.error(err);

            event.sender.send('file-read', 'Error
reading file.');

        } else {

        event.sender.send('file-read', data);

        }

    });

    }

}).catch(err => {

    console.error(err);

});

});

```
```

This code:

Imports the `ipcMain` and `dialog` modules.

Listens for the `read-file` message from the renderer process.

Uses `dialog.showOpenDialog` to allow the user to select a file.

Reads the content of the selected file using `fs.readFile`.
```

Sends the file content back to the renderer process using `event.sender.send`.

Now, when you run the application and click the "Read File" button, it will open a file dialog, and the content of the selected file will be displayed in the application window.

Important Considerations for Production

- Security: Electron applications need to be secured carefully. Be aware of the security implications of nodeIntegration and contextIsolation.
- Packaging and Distribution: Electron provides tools to package your application for different operating systems. You'll need to learn how to use these tools to create installers and distributable packages.
- Performance: Optimize your application for performance. Web technologies can sometimes be slower than native code.
- Debugging: Learn how to debug Electron applications. You can use the Chrome DevTools to debug the renderer process and Node.js debugging tools for the main process.

Electron and Node.js provide a powerful platform for building cross-platform desktop applications. By understanding the core concepts and best practices, you can create robust and feature-rich applications for a wide range of operating systems.

4.2 Mobile Development with React Native/NativeScript and Node.js

Let's explore the world of mobile development in the context of Node.js. While Node.js itself doesn't directly build the mobile user interface, it plays a vital and often indispensable role in the mobile development ecosystem. Frameworks like React Native and

NativeScript, which are popular for building cross-platform mobile applications, heavily rely on Node.js and its ecosystem.

It's important to clarify the distinction here. Node.js is not used to create the native UI components of mobile apps. Instead, it's primarily used for:

- Development Tools and Build Processes: Node.js powers many of the tools and processes involved in mobile development, such as:
    - Bundlers (like Metro in React Native): These tools package your JavaScript code and assets into a format that can be understood by the mobile device.
    - Command-line interfaces (CLIs): These tools simplify project setup, building, and deployment.
    - Package management (npm/yarn): Node.js's package managers are used to install and manage the dependencies required by mobile projects.
- Backend API Development: Node.js is exceptionally well-suited for building the backend APIs that mobile apps consume.

React Native

React Native is a popular framework for building native mobile applications using JavaScript and React. It allows developers to write code[1] once and deploy it on both iOS and Android platforms,[2] resulting in truly native mobile apps.

Node.js's Role in React Native Development

- Metro Bundler: React Native uses Metro, a JavaScript bundler written in JavaScript and runs on Node.js. Metro takes your JavaScript code, transforms it, and packages it into bundles that are then deployed to the mobile device.

- npm/yarn: These Node.js package managers are used to install React Native itself and the various libraries and dependencies required for your project.
- React Native CLI: The React Native command-line interface, which is installed via npm, provides commands for creating, building, and running React Native projects.

A Basic React Native Example

Here's a simple example of a React Native component:

JavaScript

```
import React from 'react';

import { View, Text, StyleSheet } from
'react-native';


const MyComponent = () => {

  return (

    <View style={styles.container}>

      <Text style={styles.text}>Hello, React
Native!</Text>

    </View>

  );

};


const styles = StyleSheet.create({
```

```
container: {

  flex: 1,

  justifyContent: 'center',

  alignItems: 'center',

},

text: {

  fontSize: 20,

},

});
```

```
export default MyComponent;
```

This code defines a simple component that displays the text "Hello, React Native!". React Native then compiles this code into native UI components for iOS and Android.

Node.js for Backend APIs

A common pattern is to use React Native for the mobile app's front-end and Node.js for the backend API. The mobile app then communicates with the Node.js API to retrieve and update data.

Here's a simple example of a Node.js API endpoint that a React Native app might use:

JavaScript

```
// Example Node.js API endpoint

const express = require('express');
```

```javascript
const app = express();

const port = 3000;


app.get('/api/data', (req, res) => {

    const data = { message: 'Hello from the Node.js
API!' };

    res.json(data);

});


app.listen(port, () => {

    console.log(`Server listening at
http://localhost:${port}`);

});
```

The React Native app can then use a library like fetch or axios to make HTTP requests to this API.

JavaScript

```javascript
// Example React Native code to fetch data from
the API

import React, { useState, useEffect } from
'react';

import { View, Text } from 'react-native';


const MyComponent = () => {
```

```
  const [message, setMessage] = useState('');

  useEffect(() => {
    fetch('http://localhost:3000/api/data')
      .then(response => response.json())
      .then(data => setMessage(data.message))
      .catch(error => console.error(error));
  }, []);

  return (
    <View>
      <Text>{message}</Text>
    </View>
  );
};

export default MyComponent;
```

This React Native component fetches data from the Node.js API and displays it.

NativeScript

NativeScript is another framework that allows you to build native mobile applications using JavaScript, TypeScript, or Angular. Similar to React Native, NativeScript compiles your code into native UI components, resulting in native performance and a native user experience.

Node.js plays a similar role in NativeScript development, powering the build tools, CLI, and package management.

A Practical Exercise

Let's create a simple scenario to illustrate the interaction between a React Native app and a Node.js API.

Create a Node.js API:

Create a Node.js API that returns a list of items.

For example:

```JavaScript
// Node.js API

const express = require('express');

const app = express();

const port = 3000;
```

```javascript
app.get('/api/items', (req, res) => {

  const items = [

    { id: 1, name: 'Item 1' },

    { id: 2, name: 'Item 2' },

  ];

  res.json(items);

});



app.listen(port, () => {

  console.log(`Server listening at
http://localhost:${port}`);

});
```

Create a React Native App:

Create a React Native app that fetches the list of items from the Node.js API.

Display the list of items in a FlatList.

```javascript
JavaScript



// React Native App
```

```jsx
import React, { useState, useEffect } from
'react';

import { View, Text, FlatList } from
'react-native';


const MyComponent = () => {

  const [items, setItems] = useState([]);


  useEffect(() => {

    fetch('http://localhost:3000/api/items')

      .then(response => response.json())

      .then(data => setItems(data))

      .catch(error => console.error(error));

  }, []);


  return (

    <View>

      <FlatList

        data={items}

        keyExtractor={item => item.id.toString()}

        renderItem={({ item }) =>
<Text>{item.name}</Text>}
```

```
        />

    </View>

  );

};


export default MyComponent;
```

This exercise demonstrates how Node.js and React Native work together to build a complete mobile application. Node.js provides the backend API, and React Native provides the mobile front-end.

In conclusion, Node.js plays a crucial but often behind-the-scenes role in mobile development with frameworks like React Native and NativeScript. It powers the development tools and is commonly used to build the backend APIs that these mobile apps consume.

4.3 Sharing Code Between Web and Mobile

Let's discuss a crucial aspect of cross-platform development: sharing code between web and mobile applications. In the quest for efficiency and consistency, the ability to reuse code across different platforms is a significant advantage. It can drastically reduce development time, minimize maintenance efforts, and ensure a more uniform user experience.

The challenge lies in the fact that web and mobile development often involve different technologies and paradigms. Web applications typically run in a browser and use HTML, CSS, and JavaScript, while mobile applications are often built using native or near-native technologies for each platform (e.g., Swift/Objective-C for iOS, Kotlin/Java for Android).

However, with the rise of JavaScript-based mobile frameworks and the increasing sophistication of web technologies, there are several effective strategies for sharing code between web and mobile.

Strategies for Sharing Code

Shared Libraries (Node.js Modules):

- This is a common and effective approach for sharing non-UI related logic. You can create Node.js modules that contain code that can be used by both your web and mobile applications.
- These modules typically encapsulate business logic, data manipulation functions, utility functions, or API client code.

For example, you could create a module that handles:

- Data formatting and validation.
- Date and time manipulation.
- API communication.
- Authentication and authorization logic.

Here's an example of a shared utility module:

JavaScript

```
// shared-utils.js
```

```javascript
function formatDate(date, format = 'YYYY-MM-DD')
{

  if (!date) return '';

  const dateObj = new Date(date);

  const year = dateObj.getFullYear();

  const month = String(dateObj.getMonth() +
1).padStart(2, '0');

  const day =
String(dateObj.getDate()).padStart(2, '0');

  if (format === 'YYYY-MM-DD') {

    return `<span
class="math-inline">\{year\}\-</span>{month}-${da
y}`;

  }

  // Add more format options as needed

  return `<span
class="math-inline">\{year\}\-</span>{month}-${da
y}`;

}


function isValidEmail(email) {

  if (!email) return false;

  const emailRegex =
/^[^\s@]+@[^\s@]+\.[^\s@]+\.[^\s@]+$/;
```

```
    return emailRegex.test(email);

}


module.exports = {

    formatDate,

    isValidEmail,

};
```

This module can then be imported and used in both your web and mobile applications.

Monorepos:

- A monorepo is a repository that contains multiple related projects. In a cross-platform context, a monorepo might contain both your web and mobile applications, along with shared libraries.
- Tools like Lerna or Yarn Workspaces can be used to manage dependencies and build processes within a monorepo.
- Monorepos facilitate code sharing and collaboration by keeping all related projects in a single place.

UI Component Libraries:

- While sharing UI code directly can be more challenging due to platform-specific UI components, there are strategies for sharing some UI-related code.

- For example, you can share design tokens (colors, fonts, spacing) and some basic UI logic.
- Frameworks and libraries are emerging to help with this, but it's still an evolving area.

Backend as a Shared Service:

- A common pattern is to use a Node.js backend API as a shared service for both web and mobile applications.
- This API provides the data and business logic that both the web and mobile applications consume.
- This approach maximizes code reuse on the backend and ensures consistency in data and logic.

A Practical Example: Shared Form Validation

Let's illustrate code sharing with a common scenario: form validation.

Create a Shared Validation Module:

Create a Node.js module that contains validation functions:

JavaScript

```javascript
// shared-validation.js

function validateEmail(email) {

  if (!email) return 'Email is required';
```

```javascript
  if (!/^[^\s@]+@[^\s@]+\.[^\s@]+$/.test(email))
{

    return 'Invalid email format';

  }

  return null; // Valid

}


function validatePassword(password) {

  if (!password) return 'Password is required';

  if (password.length < 8) {

    return 'Password must be at least 8
characters long';

  }

  return null; // Valid

}


module.exports = {

  validateEmail,

  validatePassword,

};
```

Use the Module in a Web Application:

In your web application, import the module and use the validation functions:

```
JavaScript
```

```javascript
// web-app.js

const validation =
require('./shared-validation');



const emailInput =
document.getElementById('email');

const passwordInput =
document.getElementById('password');

const emailError =
document.getElementById('email-error');

const passwordError =
document.getElementById('password-error');


function validateForm() {

  const email = emailInput.value;

  const password = passwordInput.value;
```

```javascript
  const emailValidation =
validation.validateEmail(email);

  const passwordValidation =
validation.validatePassword(password);


  if (emailValidation) {

    emailError.textContent = emailValidation;

  } else {

    emailError.textContent = '';

  }


  if (passwordValidation) {

    passwordError.textContent =
passwordValidation;

  } else {

    passwordError.textContent = '';

  }


  return !emailValidation && !passwordValidation;

}
```

Use the Module in a React Native Application:

In your React Native application, import the module and use the validation functions:

JavaScript

```
// react-native-app.js

import React, { useState } from 'react';

import { View, Text, TextInput, Button } from 'react-native';

import validation from './shared-validation';


const MyForm = () => {

  const [email, setEmail] = useState('');

  const [password, setPassword] = useState('');

  const [emailError, setEmailError] =
useState('');

  const [passwordError, setPasswordError] =
useState('');


  const validateForm = () => {
```

```
    const emailValidation =
validation.validateEmail(email);

    const passwordValidation =
validation.validatePassword(password);


    setEmailError(emailValidation);

    setPasswordError(passwordValidation);


    return !emailValidation &&
!passwordValidation;
  };


  return (
    <View>
      <TextInput
        placeholder="Email"
        value={email}
        onChangeText={setEmail}
      />
      {emailError && <Text style={{ color: 'red'
}}>{emailError}</Text>}
```

```
    <TextInput

      placeholder="Password"

      value={password}

      onChangeText={setPassword}

      secureTextEntry

    />

    {passwordError && <Text style={{ color:
'red' }}>{passwordError}</Text>}


    <Button title="Submit"
onPress={validateForm} />

  </View>

  );

};


export default MyForm;
```

This example demonstrates how you can share form validation logic between a web application and a React Native application using a shared Node.js module.

Sharing code between web and mobile applications is a powerful technique for improving development efficiency and consistency. By using shared libraries, monorepos, and other strategies, you can reduce code duplication and create more maintainable cross-platform applications.

Chapter 5: Native Module Interactions

While cross-platform frameworks like React Native and NativeScript allow us to write a lot of code in JavaScript, there are often situations where we need to access platform-specific features that are not directly exposed by the framework. This is where native modules come into play.

5.1 Accessing Platform-Specific Features with Native Modules

Okay, let's explore in detail how we can access platform-specific features using native modules. This is a critical aspect of cross-platform development, especially when you need to tap into the unique capabilities of each operating system.

When we talk about "platform-specific features," we're referring to functionalities that are tied to a particular operating system or device and aren't directly available through the standard APIs of cross-platform frameworks. These features often involve interacting with the underlying hardware, operating system services, or platform-specific SDKs.

Here are some examples of platform-specific features that often require native modules:

- Advanced Camera Functionality: While cross-platform frameworks might provide basic camera access, features like manual focus control, exposure settings, RAW image capture, or specialized camera modes often necessitate native code.
- Bluetooth Low Energy (BLE) Communication: Interacting with BLE devices often requires using platform-specific

Bluetooth APIs. For example, Core Bluetooth on iOS and the Bluetooth LE API on Android.

- Device Sensors: Accessing advanced sensor data beyond basic accelerometer or gyroscope readings may require native code. This could include features like barometer data, magnetometer readings, or specialized sensor fusion techniques.
- Push Notifications: Implementing push notifications often involves using platform-specific services. For iOS, you need to interact with the Apple Push Notification service (APNs), and for Android, you might use Firebase Cloud Messaging (FCM), which often requires native code integration.
- Background Tasks and Processes: Performing tasks in the background, such as data synchronization or location updates, often requires using platform-specific mechanisms for task scheduling and execution.
- Hardware Acceleration and Graphics: For performance-intensive graphics operations or hardware acceleration, you might need to use platform-specific graphics APIs like Metal on iOS or OpenGL ES on Android.

What are Native Modules?

Native modules are essentially plugins that allow us to extend the capabilities of our cross-platform applications with code written in the native language of the platform. They act as a bridge between the shared JavaScript codebase and the platform's native code.

A native module typically consists of two main parts:

Native Code Implementation:

- This is the code written in the native programming language of the target platform.

- For iOS, this is typically Objective-C or Swift. This code utilizes the iOS SDK and APIs to access the platform's features.
- For Android, this is typically Kotlin or Java. This code utilizes the Android SDK and APIs to access the platform's features.

JavaScript Bridge:

- This is the mechanism that facilitates communication between the JavaScript code and the native code.
- Cross-platform frameworks like React Native provide a bridge that enables us to call functions or methods defined in the native code from our JavaScript code.

How Native Modules Work

The typical workflow for using native modules involves the following steps:

Native Module Development:

- As a developer, you write the native code that implements the desired platform-specific functionality. This involves using the platform's SDKs and APIs.
- You define a set of functions or methods in your native code that you want to make accessible from your JavaScript environment. These functions essentially act as the interface between the native code and the JavaScript environment.

Module Registration:

- The native module needs to be registered with the cross-platform framework. This involves providing information about the module and its exposed functions to the framework.

JavaScript Integration:

- In your JavaScript code, you import or access the native module. The framework provides a way to access the native module as if it were a regular JavaScript module.
- You can then call the functions or methods exposed by the native module to access the platform-specific features.

Data Exchange:

- Data can be passed between the JavaScript code and the native code. The framework typically handles the conversion of data types between the two environments, but you might need to handle some data conversions manually.

A Conceptual Example (React Native)

Let's illustrate this with a conceptual example in React Native. Suppose we want to create a native module that provides access to the device's accelerometer.

Native Module Implementation:

iOS (Objective-C/Swift):

- We would use the Core Motion framework to access accelerometer data.
- We would create a native module with functions like startAccelerometerUpdates() and stopAccelerometerUpdates().
- We would use React Native's RCT_EXPORT_METHOD macro to expose these functions to JavaScript.

Android (Kotlin/Java):

- We would use the SensorManager class to access accelerometer data.
- We would create a native module with equivalent functions to the iOS version.
- We would use React Native's @ReactMethod annotation to expose these functions to JavaScript.

JavaScript Integration (React Native):

- In our React Native JavaScript code, we would import the native module:

```
JavaScript
```

```
import { NativeModules } from 'react-native';

const AccelerometerModule =
NativeModules.AccelerometerModule; //
Hypothetical module name
```

We can then use the functions exposed by the native module:

```
Cgbvgb FB bgccfbccbffvfbfbfbfçJavaScript
```

```
import React, { useState, useEffect } from
'react';

import { View, Text } from 'react-native';


const MyComponent = () => {

  const [acceleration, setAcceleration] =
useState({ x: 0, y: 0, z: 0 });


  useEffect(() => {

    const startUpdates = async () => {

      try {

        await
AccelerometerModule.startAccelerometerUpdates();
```

```
      // Listen for accelerometer data events
(hypothetical)

      // This part would involve using the
framework's event system

    } catch (error {

      console.error('Error starting
accelerometer updates:', error);

    }

  };


  const stopUpdates = async () => {

    try {

      await
AccelerometerModule.stopAccelerometerUpdates();

    } catch (error {

      console.error('Error stopping
accelerometer updates:', error);

    }

  };


  startUpdates();


  return () => {
```

```
        stopUpdates();

    };

  }, []);



  // ... display acceleration data ...

};
```

In this example,
AccelerometerModule.startAccelerometerUpdates() and
AccelerometerModule.stopAccelerometerUpdates() are
hypothetical functions exposed by the native module.

Important Considerations:

- Asynchronous Operations: Native module operations are often asynchronous, especially when dealing with hardware access. You'll need to use promises or callbacks to handle the results.
- Data Type Conversion: You'll need to be mindful of data type conversion between JavaScript and native code. The framework handles some of this automatically, but you might need to perform manual conversions in some cases.
- Error Handling: Implement robust error handling to deal with potential issues in the native code.

Accessing platform-specific features with native modules is a powerful technique, but it adds complexity. It's essential to use it judiciously and follow best practices to ensure a maintainable and performant codebase.

5.2 Managing Platform-Specific Dependencies

Okay, let's focus on the crucial topic of managing platform-specific dependencies. This is a challenge that cross-platform developers frequently encounter, especially when working with native modules. Effectively handling these dependencies is essential for a smooth development process and a stable application.

The Nature of Platform-Specific Dependencies

When we integrate native code to access platform features, we often have to rely on external libraries or Software Development Kits (SDKs) that are tailored for a particular operating system. These are platform-specific dependencies.

Here's a breakdown of the challenge:

- Different Dependency Management Systems: Each platform typically has its own preferred way of managing external code.
    - iOS: The standard tools are CocoaPods and Swift Package Manager.
    - Android: The standard tool is Gradle.
- Different Dependency Formats: The way these dependencies are packaged and distributed varies. iOS dependencies might be distributed as CocoaPods "Pods" or Swift Packages, while Android dependencies are typically distributed as Android Archive (AAR) files.

This means you're dealing with different systems, formats, and ways of declaring dependencies, which adds complexity to your build process and project setup.

Strategies for Effective Management

To overcome this challenge, here are some key strategies:

Embrace Platform-Specific Dependency Managers:

- The most effective approach is to utilize the standard dependency management tools for each platform. This ensures compatibility and adherence to platform conventions.

iOS: CocoaPods or Swift Package Manager

- CocoaPods is a widely used dependency manager for Objective-C and Swift projects. It simplifies the process of adding, updating, and managing external libraries. You typically define your dependencies in a Podfile.
- Swift Package Manager is Apple's native dependency management tool for Swift. It's becoming the standard for managing Swift dependencies and is well-integrated with Xcode.

Android: Gradle

- Gradle is Android's powerful build automation system. It's the standard tool for managing dependencies in Android projects. You declare your dependencies in build.gradle files.

By using these tools, you delegate the complexities of dependency resolution, downloading, and linking to the platform's standard systems.

Automated Linking and Integration:

- Some cross-platform frameworks attempt to automate the process of linking and integrating native dependencies.
- For example, React Native has a linking mechanism that, in some cases, can automatically add and configure native libraries for iOS and Android.
- However, automated linking is not always reliable, and manual configuration is often still required, especially for more complex dependencies or when dealing with specific project setups.

Clear and Comprehensive Documentation:

- When working with platform-specific dependencies, it's crucial to provide clear and detailed documentation for your project.

This documentation should include:

- Instructions on installing and configuring the necessary dependency managers (CocoaPods, Gradle, etc.).
- Specific instructions on adding the required dependencies to the platform-specific configuration files (Podfile for CocoaPods, build.gradle for Gradle).

- Any manual linking or configuration steps that may be required, including screenshots or detailed command-line instructions.
- This documentation should be tailored to each platform and provide step-by-step guidance.

Dependency Versioning and Compatibility:

- Careful attention must be paid to dependency versioning. Ensure that the versions of your native dependencies are compatible with:
    - Your cross-platform framework (e.g., React Native).
    - Your native module code.
    - Other dependencies in your project.
    - Conflicts between dependency versions can lead to a range of problems, including:
        - Build errors
        - Runtime crashes
        - Unexpected behavior
    - Use the dependency management tools to specify version constraints and resolve potential conflicts.

Modular Design and Isolation:

- A modular design approach can significantly simplify dependency management.
- Try to encapsulate platform-specific dependencies within individual native modules.
- For example, if you have a native module that uses a particular Bluetooth library, try to isolate that dependency within the module's code. This makes it easier to:
    - Update or replace the dependency in the future.

- Test the module in isolation.
- Reduce the risk of dependency conflicts with other parts of your project.

A Practical Example (React Native)

Let's illustrate dependency management with a React Native example where you need to integrate a native library for image processing.

iOS (CocoaPods):

Create a Podfile in your ios directory:

Ruby

```ruby
# Podfile
platform :ios, '11.0'

target 'YourAppName' do
  # ... other pods ...
  pod 'MyImageProcessingLibrary', '~> 1.2.0'
end
```

Run pod install in the ios directory to install the dependency.

Android (Gradle):

Add the dependency to your build.gradle file in the android/app directory:

Gradle

```
// build.gradle (Module: app)

dependencies {

  // ... other dependencies ...

  implementation
'com.mycompany:myimageprocessinglibrary:1.0.0'

}
```

Sync your Gradle project in Android Studio to download and link the dependency.

Documentation:

- Your project documentation should clearly explain these platform-specific steps, including:
  - Installing CocoaPods (if necessary) on iOS.
  - Adding the pod line to the Podfile.
  - Adding the implementation line to the build.gradle file.
  - Running pod install on iOS and syncing Gradle on Android.

By consistently applying these strategies, you can effectively manage platform-specific dependencies, ensuring a more organized, efficient, and stable cross-platform development workflow.

5.3 Best Practices for Native Module Integration

Okay, let's talk about best practices for native module integration. When you're working with native modules in cross-platform development, you're essentially bridging the gap between two different codebases and technologies. It's crucial to approach this integration with care to ensure a stable, maintainable, and efficient application.

Here are some essential best practices to follow:

Minimize Native Code Usage:

- Native code adds complexity to your project. It requires platform-specific knowledge, increases maintenance overhead, and can introduce potential bugs or performance issues.
- Therefore, a core principle should be to use native modules only when absolutely necessary.
- Before resorting to native code, explore alternative solutions using JavaScript or the features provided by your cross-platform framework.
- For example, if you need to perform a simple image manipulation, consider using a JavaScript library instead of writing a native module.

Design Clear and Consistent Interfaces:

- When you do need to create native modules, design clear and consistent interfaces for them.
- Think of these interfaces as contracts between your JavaScript code and your native code.
- Define a set of functions or methods that your native module will expose to JavaScript.
- Ensure that these functions have well-defined input parameters and return values.
- Use consistent naming conventions and data types.
- This will make your native modules easier to use and understand from JavaScript.

Abstraction Layers (When Appropriate):

- In some cases, it can be beneficial to create abstraction layers to hide platform-specific details from your JavaScript code.
- This is particularly useful when dealing with functionalities that have significant platform differences.
- For example, if you need to access the device's file system, you might create an abstraction layer that provides a common set of file access functions. Under the hood, this abstraction layer would use platform-specific code (e.g., File API for web, native modules for mobile) to perform the file operations.
- Abstraction layers can improve code portability and maintainability, but they also add an extra layer of complexity. Use them judiciously.

Asynchronous Operations and Error Handling:

- Native module operations are often asynchronous, especially when dealing with hardware access or complex system calls.
- Ensure that you handle asynchronous operations correctly using promises, callbacks, or async/await.
- Implement robust error handling to deal with potential issues in the native code.
- Propagate errors from the native code to the JavaScript environment in a clear and consistent way.
- Provide informative error messages that can help with debugging.

Data Type Conversion and Marshalling:

- Be mindful of data type conversion between JavaScript and native code.
- Cross-platform frameworks often handle some data type conversions automatically, but you might need to perform manual conversions in certain cases.
- For example, you might need to convert JavaScript objects into native data structures or vice versa.
- Pay close attention to data types like strings, numbers, arrays, and objects.

Thorough Testing on Each Platform:

- Native modules inherently involve platform-specific code, which means they need to be tested thoroughly on each target platform.

- Don't assume that your native module will work correctly on all platforms just because it works on one.
- Pay attention to edge cases, potential compatibility issues, and performance differences.
- Use device emulators, simulators, and real devices for testing.

Documentation is Key:

- Document your native modules clearly and comprehensively.
- Include instructions on:
  - Installation and setup (including platform-specific dependencies).
  - Usage of each exposed function or method.
  - Data types and expected input/output.
  - Error handling.
  - Any platform-specific considerations or limitations.
  - Good documentation will make your native modules easier to use and maintain.

Leverage Community Modules (When Possible):

- Before writing your own native module from scratch, check if there's a well-maintained community module that already provides the functionality you need.
- The community often provides high-quality modules that are well-tested and optimized.
- Using community modules can save you time and effort.
- However, carefully evaluate the quality and maintenance status of any community module before relying on it.

By adhering to these best practices, you can effectively integrate native modules into your cross-platform applications, ensuring a robust, maintainable, and performant codebase.

Chapter 6: Build Automation and Continuous Integration

In this chapter, we'll explore how to automate the build process for different platforms, set up CI/CD pipelines to streamline development, and leverage Docker for cross-platform deployment. These techniques will help you improve efficiency, reduce errors, and ensure a smooth release process.

6.1 Automating Builds for Different Platforms

Let's discuss automating builds for different platforms. This is a fundamental aspect of modern software development, and its importance is amplified when dealing with cross-platform applications. When you're targeting multiple operating systems and environments, a manual build process quickly becomes unsustainable.

Imagine having to manually compile your code, bundle assets, and create platform-specific packages every time you make a change. It's time-consuming, error-prone, and hinders productivity. That's where build automation comes in.

What is Build Automation?

Build automation involves using tools and scripts to automate the series of steps required to transform your source code into deployable artifacts for each target platform. This process can be quite involved, depending on the complexity of your application and the platforms you're targeting.

Here's a breakdown of the typical steps that are often automated:

Code Compilation and Transpilation:

- This might involve compiling native code (e.g., C++, Swift, Kotlin) into machine code.
- It also often includes transpiling JavaScript (e.g., using Babel or TypeScript) to ensure compatibility with different browsers or environments.

Dependency Management:

- Automating the installation and linking of external libraries and dependencies.
- This is crucial for ensuring that your application has all the necessary components to run correctly.

Asset Processing:

- Optimizing and processing assets like images, CSS, and fonts.
- This might involve minifying CSS, compressing images, or bundling assets into a single file.

Packaging and Bundling:

- Creating the final distributable packages for each platform.
- This could involve generating executables (e.g., .exe files for Windows), app bundles (e.g., .app files for macOS or .apk files for Android), or web distributions.

Code Signing:

- Digitally signing your applications to verify their authenticity and integrity.
- This is often a requirement for distributing applications on app stores or to ensure security.

Testing:

- Automating the execution of tests to ensure code quality and prevent regressions.
- This can include unit tests, integration tests, and end-to-end tests.

Tools and Techniques for Build Automation

Several tools and techniques can be used to automate the build process in cross-platform development:

Task Runners:

- These tools allow you to define and execute a sequence of tasks.

Examples include:

- npm scripts: You can define build tasks directly in your package.json file.
- Gulp: A JavaScript task runner that uses code-over-configuration.
- Grunt: Another JavaScript task runner that uses a configuration-based approach.

Build Tools:

- These are platform-specific tools that are often integrated into the automation process.

Examples include:

- Xcodebuild: A command-line tool for building iOS and macOS applications.
- Gradle: Android's build automation tool.
- Electron Builder: A tool specifically designed for building Electron applications for different platforms.

Cross-Platform Build Tools:

- These tools can help automate builds for multiple platforms, simplifying the process.

Examples include:

- Fastlane: A popular tool for automating iOS and Android deployments, including code signing and app store submission.
- Electron Builder: As mentioned before, it's very useful for building Electron applications for various desktop platforms.

A Simple Example with npm Scripts

Let's illustrate build automation with a simple example using npm scripts for a web application:

JSON

```json
// package.json
{
  "scripts": {
    "build:js": "webpack --mode production",
    "build:css": "postcss styles.css -o
dist/styles.css",
    "build:html": "copy index.html
dist/index.html",
    "build": "npm run build:js && npm run
build:css && npm run build:html",
    "clean": "rm -rf dist"
  },
  "devDependencies": {
    "webpack": "^5.x.x",
    "postcss-cli": "^10.x.x",
    "copyfiles": "^2.x.x",
    "rimraf": "^5.x.x"
    // ... other dev dependencies ...
  }
}
```

In this example:

- build:js: This script uses Webpack to bundle and optimize JavaScript files for production.
- build:css: This script uses PostCSS to process CSS files.
- build:html: This script copies the HTML file to the distribution directory.
- build: This script orchestrates the other build scripts, running them sequentially to build the entire web application.
- clean: This script uses rimraf to remove the distribution directory, ensuring a clean build.

You can then execute these scripts using the npm run <script-name> command.

A More Complex Cross-Platform Scenario

For a more complex cross-platform scenario, such as building a React Native application, you might use a combination of tools:

- npm scripts to trigger the React Native CLI for building the mobile app.
- Fastlane to automate iOS and Android deployments, including code signing and app store submission.

A Practical Exercise

Let's create a practical exercise to solidify your understanding of build automation.

1. Choose a Project:
   - Select a simple web application or a basic React Native project.
2. Define Build Steps:
   - Identify the essential steps required to build your application for your target platform(s).

This might include:

- Transpiling JavaScript (if needed).
- Bundling assets (CSS, images, etc.).
- Generating platform-specific files.
3. Automate with npm Scripts:
   - Use npm scripts to automate these build steps.
   - Create individual scripts for each step and a main "build" script to orchestrate them.
4. Test Your Automation:
   - Run your build scripts and verify that they produce the correct output.

By automating your build process, you can significantly improve your development workflow, reduce errors, and ensure consistent builds across different platforms.

6.2 Setting up CI/CD Pipelines

Alright, let's talk about setting up CI/CD pipelines. This is a crucial practice in modern software development, and it becomes even more critical when you're working on cross-platform applications. CI/CD helps you automate the build, test, and deployment process, making your development workflow more efficient, reliable, and faster.

What is CI/CD?

CI/CD stands for Continuous Integration and Continuous Delivery/Continuous Deployment. It's a set of practices that aim to automate and streamline the software development lifecycle, from code changes to production releases.

- Continuous Integration (CI): This practice focuses on integrating code changes from multiple developers into a shared repository frequently. CI involves automating the build and testing process every time code is committed to the repository. This helps to detect errors early and prevent integration issues.

- Continuous Delivery (CD): This practice extends CI by automating the process of preparing code changes for release. This might involve generating build artifacts, running automated tests, and staging the changes in a pre-production environment.
- Continuous Deployment (CD): This takes CD a step further by automating the entire release process, including deploying code changes to production.

Why is CI/CD Important for Cross-Platform Development?

CI/CD is particularly important for cross-platform development because it helps you:

- Ensure Code Quality Across Platforms: When you're building applications for multiple platforms, you need to ensure that your code works correctly on each one. CI/CD pipelines can automate the execution of tests on different platforms, giving you confidence that your code is consistent and reliable.
- Detect Platform-Specific Errors Early: CI/CD helps you catch platform-specific errors early in the development process. This can save you a lot of time and effort in the long run, as you won't be discovering these issues late in the development cycle.
- Speed Up Delivery of Updates: Automating the build, test, and deployment process allows you to release new features and bug fixes more frequently and reliably. This is especially important in the fast-paced mobile development environment.

- Improve Collaboration: CI/CD pipelines provide a centralized and automated way to manage the software development process. This can improve collaboration among developers, testers, and operations teams.

Key Components of a CI/CD Pipeline

A typical CI/CD pipeline consists of several key components:

- Version Control System: This is where your code is stored and managed. Popular version control systems include Git (used by services like GitHub, GitLab, and Bitbucket).
- CI/CD Server: This is the tool that orchestrates the automated build, test, and deployment process.

Examples of CI/CD servers include:

- Jenkins: An open-source automation server.
- GitLab CI/CD: A CI/CD service integrated into GitLab.
- GitHub Actions: A CI/CD service integrated into GitHub.
- CircleCI: A cloud-based CI/CD platform.

Build Agents

These are servers or virtual machines that execute the build, test, and deployment jobs defined in your CI/CD pipeline.

Stages of a CI/CD Pipeline

A typical CI/CD pipeline might consist of the following stages:

Code Commit:

- The pipeline is triggered when a developer pushes code changes to the version control system (e.g., a branch in Git).

Build:

- The CI/CD server pulls the latest code from the repository and executes the automated build process.

This might involve:

- Compiling source code.
- Transpiling JavaScript.
- Bundling assets.
- Generating platform-specific artifacts (e.g., APKs, IPAs, executables).

Test:

- Automated tests are executed to verify the code changes.

This might include:

- Unit tests.

- Integration tests.
- End-to-end tests.
- UI tests (for mobile applications).

Artifacts:

- If the build and tests are successful, the CI/CD pipeline generates deployable artifacts for each target platform.

Deployment:

- The artifacts are deployed to the target environments.

This might involve:

- Deploying to a staging environment for further testing.
- Deploying to a production environment for release to users.
- Uploading to app stores (for mobile applications).

A Conceptual Example (GitHub Actions)

Let's illustrate a CI/CD pipeline for a React Native application using GitHub Actions:

YAML

```yaml
# .github/workflows/ci-cd.yml

name: CI/CD
```

```
on:

  push:

    branches:

      - main


jobs:

  build_test:

    runs-on: ubuntu-latest

    steps:

      - uses: actions/checkout@v3 # Checkout the
code

      - uses: actions/setup-node@v3 # Setup
Node.js

        with:

          node-version: 18

      - run: npm install # Install dependencies

      - run: npm test # Run tests

      - run: npm run build:android # Build
Android app

      - run: npm run build:ios # Build iOS app

  deploy:
```

```
    needs: build_test

    runs-on: ubuntu-latest

    steps:

      - uses: actions/checkout@v3 # Checkout the
code

      - uses: actions/setup-node@v3 # Setup
Node.js

        with:

          node-version: 18

      - run: npm install # Install dependencies

      - run: npm run deploy:android # Deploy
Android app to store

      - run: npm run deploy:ios # Deploy iOS app
to store
```

In this example:

- The pipeline is triggered on pushes to the main branch.
- It defines two jobs: build_test and deploy.
- The build_test job runs on an Ubuntu runner and performs the build and test steps for both Android and iOS.
- The deploy job depends on the build_test job and handles the deployment of the built apps.

A Practical Exercise

Let's do a practical exercise to get you started with CI/CD:

Choose a CI/CD Service:

- Select a CI/CD service like GitHub Actions, GitLab CI/CD, or CircleCI.

Create a Simple Project:

- Choose a simple web application or a basic React Native project.

Define a Pipeline Workflow:

- Outline the steps you want to automate in your pipeline, including:
  - Code checkout.
  - Dependency installation.
  - Build process.
  - Testing.

Configure the CI/CD Pipeline:

- Create a configuration file for your chosen CI/CD service (e.g., a .gitlab-ci.yml file for GitLab CI/CD, a workflow file for GitHub Actions).
- Define the jobs, stages, and steps in your pipeline.

Test the Pipeline:

- Commit and push your code changes to trigger the pipeline.
- Monitor the pipeline execution and verify that it runs correctly.

By setting up CI/CD pipelines, you automate your software development process, improve code quality, and speed up the delivery of your cross-platform applications.

6.3 Using Docker for Cross-Platform Deployment

Okay, let's explore how Docker can be leveraged for cross-platform deployment. Docker has become a powerful tool in modern software development, and its benefits are particularly relevant when dealing with the complexities of cross-platform applications.

What is Docker?

At its core, Docker is a containerization platform. It allows you to package an application and all its dependencies into a single, lightweight, and portable unit called a container.

Think of containers as isolated environments that can run consistently across different operating systems and infrastructures.

They encapsulate everything an application needs to run, including:

- Code
- Runtime
- System tools
- System libraries

- Settings

This isolation is key to Docker's power. It eliminates the "it works on my machine" problem and ensures that your application behaves consistently regardless of where it's deployed.

Why is Docker Useful for Cross-Platform Deployment?

Docker offers several advantages that are particularly beneficial for cross-platform deployment:

Consistency Across Environments:

- Cross-platform applications often need to run on different operating systems and infrastructures.
- For example, your backend API might need to run on Linux servers, while your development environment might be macOS or Windows.
- Docker ensures consistency by packaging your application and its dependencies into a container that can run on any system with Docker installed.
- This eliminates environment-related issues and ensures that your application behaves the same way in development, staging, and production.

Simplified Deployment:

- Docker simplifies the deployment process by providing a standard way to package and distribute applications.
- Instead of dealing with platform-specific deployment procedures, you can deploy Docker containers to any environment that supports Docker.
- This makes deployment more efficient and reduces the risk of errors.

Dependency Management:

- Docker containers include all the necessary dependencies, so you don't have to worry about installing them on the target environment.
- This is especially useful for cross-platform applications that might have dependencies on specific system libraries or tools.
- Docker ensures that your application has all the required dependencies to run correctly, regardless of the target environment.

Scalability and Portability:

- Docker containers are lightweight and portable, making it easy to scale your applications and move them between different environments.
- You can easily run multiple instances of your application in Docker containers, which is useful for scaling your application to handle increased traffic.
- You can also easily move your Docker containers between different cloud providers or on-premises servers.

How to Use Docker for Cross-Platform Deployment

Here's a general approach to using Docker for cross-platform deployment:

Containerize Your Application:

- Create a Dockerfile that defines how to build a Docker image for your application.

- The Dockerfile specifies the base image to use, the dependencies to install, the code to copy, and the command to run the application.

Build Docker Images:

- Use the docker build command to create Docker images from your Dockerfiles.
- You might create separate Dockerfiles for different parts of your application (e.g., backend API, web frontend).

Run Docker Containers:

- Use the docker run command to start Docker containers from your Docker images.
- You can run Docker containers on your local development machine, on staging servers, or in production environments.

Orchestrate Containers (for complex applications):

- For more complex applications that consist of multiple containers, you can use container orchestration tools like Docker Compose or Kubernetes.
- These tools allow you to define and manage the relationships between your containers.

A Simple Dockerfile Example (Node.js API)

Let's illustrate how to use Docker with a simple Node.js API:

```
Dockerfile

# Use a Node.js base image

FROM node:18-alpine


# Set the working directory

WORKDIR /app


# Copy package.json and package-lock.json

COPY package*.json ./


# Install dependencies

RUN npm install


# Copy the application code

COPY . .


# Expose the port

EXPOSE 3000


# Start the application
```

```
CMD [ "npm", "start" ]
```

Explanation:

- FROM node:18-alpine: This line specifies the base image to use. We're using a lightweight Node.js image based on Alpine Linux.
- WORKDIR /app: This sets the working directory inside the container to /app.
- COPY package*.json ./: This copies the package.json and package-lock.json files to the working directory.
- RUN npm install: This installs the dependencies specified in package.json.
- COPY . .: This copies the entire application code to the working directory.
- EXPOSE 3000: This exposes port 3000, which is the port that our Node.js API will listen on.
- CMD ["npm", "start"]: This specifies the command to run when the container starts.

A Practical Exercise

Let's do a practical exercise to get you started with Docker:

Create a Simple Node.js API:

- If you don't already have one, create a very basic Node.js API that returns a simple JSON response.

Create a Dockerfile:

- Create a Dockerfile for your Node.js API, similar to the example above.

Build a Docker Image:

- Use the docker build command to build a Docker image from your Dockerfile:

Bash

```bash
docker build -t my-nodejs-api .
```

Run a Docker Container:

- Use the docker run command to run a Docker container from your image:

Bash

```bash
docker run -p 3000:3000 my-nodejs-api
```

Test Your API:

- Access your API through your browser or a tool like curl to verify that it's working correctly.

By using Docker, you can significantly simplify the deployment of your cross-platform applications, ensuring consistency and portability across different environments.

Chapter 7: Packaging and Distribution

In this chapter, we'll guide you through the process of taking your built application and preparing it for delivery to your users. This involves creating installers, app bundles, and handling the unique requirements of each platform.

7.1 Packaging Applications for Windows, macOS, and Linux

Let's explore the essential process of packaging applications for the three major desktop operating systems: Windows, macOS, and Linux. This is a crucial step in the software development lifecycle, as it determines how your application is delivered to and installed by end-users. Each platform has its own conventions and requirements, so understanding these nuances is key to a successful release.

When we talk about "packaging," we're referring to the process of taking your application's files (including executables, libraries, assets, and other resources) and bundling them into a format that's suitable for distribution and installation on a specific operating system. This process is more than just zipping files; it involves creating installers or application bundles that adhere to the platform's standards.

Windows Packaging

Windows applications are typically distributed as executable installer files, which users run to install the application on their systems. These installers often have a .exe file extension.

Installer Tools:

- To create Windows installers, developers commonly use specialized tools that simplify the process.

Some popular choices include:

- Inno Setup: This is a free installer for Windows applications. It's known for its powerful scripting capabilities, allowing developers to create highly customized installers. Inno Setup supports features like:
  - Selecting an installation directory.
  - Creating shortcuts on the desktop and start menu.
  - Registering file associations (e.g., making your application the default program to open certain file types).
  - Handling uninstallation, including removing files and registry entries.

NSIS (Nullsoft Scriptable Install System)

This is another free and open-source installer system for Windows. It's also script-driven and provides a wide range of features.

Installer Functionality:

- Windows installers typically guide users through the installation process in a step-by-step manner.

Common installer functions include:

- License Agreement: Displaying and requiring acceptance of a software license agreement.
- Installation Directory Selection: Allowing users to choose where the application should be installed.
- Component Selection: In some cases, installers allow users to choose which components of the application they want to install.
- Shortcut Creation: Creating shortcuts on the desktop and in the Start Menu for easy access to the application.
- File Associations: Registering the application to handle specific file types.
- Uninstallation: Providing a mechanism for users to easily uninstall the application and remove its files.

Code Signing:

- Code signing is a crucial security practice for Windows applications. It involves digitally signing your application with a code signing certificate.
- A code signing certificate is issued by a trusted Certificate Authority (CA) and verifies the authenticity and integrity of your application.
- Code signing helps to:

- Establish trust with users by confirming that the application comes from a known and trusted source.
- Prevent security warnings that might be displayed by Windows SmartScreen, a feature that helps protect users from malicious software.

macOS Packaging

macOS applications are typically distributed as application bundles or packaged installers.

Application Bundles (.app):

- Application bundles are self-contained directories that have a .app extension.
- These bundles contain all the files and resources that an application needs to run, including:
  - Executables
  - Libraries
  - Assets (images, sounds, etc.)
  - Metadata
- macOS users are often accustomed to installing applications by simply dragging and dropping the .app file from a disk image (.dmg file) into their Applications folder.

Package Installers (.pkg):

- Package installers are used for more complex installations or when you need to install components outside of the application bundle.
- For example, you might use a package installer if you need to:
  - Install command-line tools in a system directory.

- Install frameworks or libraries that need to be accessible to other applications.
- Perform system-level configuration.

Code Signing:

- Code signing is also essential for macOS applications.
- Apple requires that applications be signed with an Apple Developer ID certificate to be distributed.
- Code signing helps to:
    - Verify the identity of the developer.
    - Prevent unauthorized modifications to the application.
    - Meet Apple's security requirements for macOS applications.

Linux Packaging

Linux application distribution is more fragmented compared to Windows or macOS. There isn't a single, universally accepted format for packaging applications. This is due to the diverse nature of Linux distributions.

Common Distribution Formats:

- Here are some of the most common formats used for distributing Linux applications:

Debian packages (.deb)

These packages are used by Debian-based distributions, which include popular distributions like Ubuntu, Debian, and Linux Mint.

RPM packages (.rpm)

These packages are used by Red Hat-based distributions, such as Fedora, CentOS, and Red Hat Enterprise Linux.

AppImage

This is a format that packages an application and all its dependencies into a single file. AppImage aims to be distribution-agnostic, meaning that an AppImage should be able to run on most Linux distributions.

Snap

This is a package format developed by Canonical (the company behind Ubuntu). Snaps are designed to work across a wide range of Linux distributions.

Flatpak

This is another distribution-agnostic package format that aims to provide a consistent way to distribute applications on Linux.

Distribution Strategy:

- The best distribution strategy for Linux depends on your target audience and the distributions they are likely to use.
- You might need to provide packages in multiple formats to reach a wider audience.
- Alternatively, you can focus on a distribution-agnostic format like AppImage, Snap, or Flatpak.

Code Signing:

- While not as strictly enforced as on Windows or macOS, code signing is still a good practice for Linux applications.
- It can help to verify the integrity of your application and prevent tampering.

Electron and Packaging Tools

If you're building desktop applications with Electron, tools like Electron Builder or Electron Packager can automate the packaging process for different platforms. These tools simplify the process of creating installers or application bundles for Windows, macOS, and Linux.

A Practical Exercise

To gain a practical understanding of packaging, I recommend the following exercise:

1. Choose a Target Platform: Select either Windows, macOS, or Linux.
2. Research Packaging Tools: Research the specific tools and formats used for packaging applications on your chosen platform (e.g., Inno Setup for Windows, creating an .app bundle for macOS, or AppImage for Linux).
3. Package a Simple Application: If you have a simple desktop application (even a basic one created with Electron), try packaging it for your chosen platform. Follow the documentation and tutorials for the packaging tools you've researched.
4. Explore Code Signing: Investigate the code signing process for your chosen platform. Understand how to obtain a code signing certificate and how to integrate it into your packaging process.

By understanding the platform-specific requirements and using the appropriate tools, you can effectively package your desktop applications for distribution to a wider audience.

7.2 *Distributing Mobile Apps (iOS and Android)*

Let's explore the process of distributing mobile applications, focusing on the two dominant mobile platforms: iOS and Android. This is the crucial final stage of mobile app development, where your app is made available to users.[1] Each platform has its own distinct distribution process and requirements, so understanding these differences is essential for a successful launch.

iOS App Distribution

iOS apps are distributed primarily through the Apple App Store, Apple's official app marketplace for iOS devices.[2]

Apple Developer Program:

- To distribute iOS apps, you must be a member of the Apple Developer Program.[3] This program provides access to Apple's developer tools, resources, and distribution channels.[4]

App Store Connect:

- App Store Connect is a web-based portal provided by Apple that allows developers to:[5]
    - Manage their apps.
    - Submit apps for review.
    - Release apps to the App Store.
    - Track app performance.

Distribution Process:

- The iOS app distribution process involves several key steps:

Creating an App Store Connect Record:

- You'll need to create a record for your app in App Store Connect.[6] This involves providing essential information about your app, such as:

- App name
- Description
- Category
- Price

Configuring App Metadata:

- You'll need to configure your app's metadata, which includes:
    - App name and description
    - Keywords for search optimization
    - Screenshots and app previews
    - Support URLs
    - Privacy policy
- This metadata is crucial for users to discover and understand your app.[7]

Building Your App for Release:

- You'll need to build your app for release, which involves:
- Optimizing your code
- Configuring build settings
- Generating the necessary app archive

Archiving Your App in Xcode:

- Xcode, Apple's integrated development environment (IDE), is typically used to archive your app.[8]
- Archiving creates a special build of your app that's suitable for submission to the App Store.[9]

Uploading Your App Archive to App Store Connect:

- You'll upload your app archive to App Store Connect.
- This is often done through Xcode or using Apple's command-line tools.

App Store Review Process:

- Apple has a review process to ensure that apps meet its quality and security guidelines.[10]
- Your app will undergo review by Apple's app review team.[11]
- This process can take some time, and you might need to address any issues raised by the review team.

App Release:

- Once your app passes the review, you can release it to the App Store.[12]
- You can choose to release it immediately or schedule it for a later date.

Code Signing:

- Code signing is mandatory for iOS apps.[13] It's a security mechanism that helps to:
  - Verify the identity of the app's developer.
  - Ensure that the app has not been tampered with.
  -
  - You'll need to use Apple Developer Program certificates and provisioning profiles to sign your app.[14]
  - Provisioning profiles are files that authorize your app to run on specific devices or to use certain capabilities.[15]

Android App Distribution

Android apps are primarily distributed through the Google Play Store, Google's official app marketplace for Android devices.[16]

Google Play Developer Account:

- To publish apps on the Google Play Store, you'll need a Google Play Developer account.[17]

Google Play Console:

- The Google Play Console is a web-based portal provided by Google that allows developers to:[18]
  - Manage their apps.
  - Upload and release apps.
  - Track app performance.
  -

Distribution Process:

- The Android app distribution process involves the following key steps:

Creating a Google Play Console Entry:

- You'll need to create an entry for your app in the Google Play Console.[19]
- This involves providing information about your app, such as:
  - App name
  - Description
  - Category
  - Pricing

Configuring App Details:

- You'll need to configure your app's details, which include:
  - App name and description
  - Graphics and screenshots
  - Privacy policy
  - Contact information
- This information is used to present your app to users on the Play Store.

Building Your App for Release:

- You'll need to build your app for release.
- This typically involves generating an Android Package Kit (APK) file or an Android App Bundle (AAB).[20]
- AAB is the recommended format for new apps, as it allows Google Play to optimize app delivery to different devices.[21]

Uploading Your App to the Google Play Console:

- You'll upload your app's APK or AAB file to the Google Play Console.

Google Play Review Process:

- Google Play also has an app review process, although it's generally less stringent than Apple's.[22]
- Google Play uses automated and manual checks to ensure app quality and compliance.[23]

App Release:

- Once your app meets Google Play's requirements, you can release it to the Play Store.
- You can choose to release it immediately or use staged rollouts to gradually release it to users.[24]

App Signing:

- Android apps need to be signed with a digital certificate.[25]
- This certificate is used to verify the app's authenticity and ensure that it hasn't been tampered with.
- You'll need to generate a signing key and use it to sign your app.

A Practical Exercise

To gain a practical understanding of mobile app distribution, I recommend the following exercise:

1. Choose a Target Platform: Select either iOS or Android.
2. Research the App Store/Play Store Submission Process: Research the detailed steps involved in submitting an app to the Apple App Store or the Google Play Store.
3. Create a Submission Checklist: Create a checklist of all the requirements and steps you need to complete to successfully submit an app to your chosen app store.
4. Explore Code Signing/App Signing: Investigate the code signing process for iOS or the app signing process for Android. Understand how to obtain the necessary certificates or keys and how to integrate them into your build process.

By understanding the platform-specific requirements and processes, you can effectively distribute your mobile apps to a global audience.

7.3 Strategies for Handling Platform-Specific Deployment

Okay, let's discuss strategies for handling platform-specific deployment. This is a critical aspect of cross-platform development, as you'll often encounter unique challenges and requirements when deploying your applications to different operating systems and environments.

When deploying cross-platform applications, you're essentially dealing with the final stage of the software development lifecycle, where your application is prepared and delivered to its intended users. This process can be more complex than deploying to a single platform because you need to consider the specific needs of each target environment.

Here are some key strategies to effectively handle platform-specific deployment:

Conditional Deployment Logic:

- Often, your deployment process will need to adapt to the specific platform you're targeting. This is where conditional deployment logic comes into play.
- You might need to execute different scripts, run different commands, or use different tools depending on whether you're deploying to Windows, macOS, Linux, iOS, or Android.

For example:

- You might need to use different code signing tools or certificates for each platform.
- You might need to package your application in different formats (e.g., .exe for Windows, .app for macOS, .apk for Android).
- You might need to configure environment variables differently for each platform.
- To implement conditional deployment logic, you can use:
  - Environment variables: These allow you to store platform-specific settings and access them in your deployment scripts.
  - Conditional statements: You can use programming logic within your deployment scripts to execute different actions based on the target platform.

Environment Variables:

- Environment variables play a crucial role in managing platform-specific deployment settings.
- They allow you to externalize configuration values that might vary between different environments (development, testing, production) or platforms.
- Examples of settings that might be stored in environment variables include:
  - API keys
  - App identifiers (e.g., bundle IDs for iOS, package names for Android)
  - Code signing certificates and passwords
  - Database connection strings
  - Deployment URLs
  - By using environment variables, you can:
    - Avoid hardcoding sensitive information in your deployment scripts.
    - Easily switch between different configurations without modifying your code.
    - Adapt your deployment process to different platforms and environments.

CI/CD Integration for Platform-Specific Steps:

- Continuous Integration/Continuous Delivery (CI/CD) pipelines can be configured to handle platform-specific deployment steps.
- CI/CD tools often provide features to define separate jobs or stages in your pipeline for each target platform.
- This allows you to automate the build, test, and deployment process for each platform independently.

For example:

- You might have a CI/CD job that builds and packages your application for Windows.
- You might have another job that builds and deploys your Android app to the Google Play Store.
- CI/CD tools often provide platform-specific integrations or plugins that can simplify the deployment process, such as:
    - Tools for code signing iOS and Android apps.
    - Tools for interacting with app stores.
    - Tools for deploying to different cloud platforms.

Deployment Automation Tools:

- In addition to general CI/CD tools, there are also specialized tools that can automate many of the deployment steps for specific platforms, particularly for mobile apps.
- Fastlane: This is a popular tool for automating iOS and Android app deployments. It can automate tasks like:
    - Code signing
    - Building your app for release
    - Taking screenshots
    - Uploading your app to the App Store or Google Play Store
    - Managing app metadata
- Tools like Fastlane can significantly simplify the deployment process for mobile apps, saving you time and effort.

A Practical Example (Cross-Platform Mobile App)

Let's consider a practical example of handling platform-specific deployment for a cross-platform mobile app built with React Native:

Conditional Deployment Logic:

- You might use environment variables to specify the app store credentials for iOS and Android.
- Your deployment scripts would use conditional statements to determine which code signing certificates and provisioning profiles to use based on the target platform.

Environment Variables:

- You might store the following information in environment variables:
    - IOS_APP_STORE_CONNECT_API_KEY
    - IOS_TEAM_ID
    - ANDROID_GOOGLE_PLAY_CREDENTIALS
    - ANDROID_KEYSTORE_FILE
    - ANDROID_KEYSTORE_PASSWORD

CI/CD Integration:

- Your CI/CD pipeline might have separate jobs for iOS and Android deployment.
- The iOS job would use Xcodebuild and Apple's command-line tools to build and upload the app to App Store Connect.

- The Android job would use Gradle to build and upload the app to the Google Play Store.

Deployment Automation Tools:

- You could use Fastlane to automate the code signing, building, and uploading process for both iOS and Android.

By implementing these strategies, you can effectively handle the challenges of platform-specific deployment, ensuring a smooth and successful release of your cross-platform applications.

Chapter 8: Performance Optimization

In this chapter, we'll focus on strategies and techniques to ensure that your cross-platform applications deliver a smooth and responsive user experience. We'll cover identifying performance bottlenecks, optimizing Node.js for different environments, and employing profiling and debugging tools.

8.1 Identifying Performance Bottlenecks in Cross-Platform Apps

Okay, let's talk in detail about identifying performance bottlenecks in cross-platform applications. This is a critical first step in optimizing your application and ensuring a smooth user experience across different platforms.

When developing for a single platform, you might have a clearer understanding of the performance characteristics and limitations. However, cross-platform development introduces additional complexities. Your application needs to perform well on diverse hardware, operating systems, and environments.[1] Therefore, a systematic approach to identifying potential bottlenecks is essential.

Understanding the Sources of Performance Issues

Performance bottlenecks in cross-platform applications can stem from various sources.[2]

It's crucial to consider these potential areas:

JavaScript Performance:

- JavaScript, while being the cornerstone of many cross-platform frameworks, can become a performance bottleneck if not handled carefully.
- Inefficient JavaScript code can lead to:
  - Slow execution: Code that takes a long time to run, causing delays or unresponsive UI.
  - Excessive memory consumption: Code that uses up a lot of memory, potentially leading to crashes or slowdowns.
  - UI lag: Slow JavaScript code can block the main thread, causing the user interface to become choppy or unresponsive.[3]
- This is especially relevant in complex applications with heavy computations or animations.

Rendering Performance:

- Rendering performance is a critical factor in both web and mobile applications.[4] It dictates how smoothly and quickly the user interface is displayed.
- Slow rendering can result in:
  - Choppy animations: Animations that appear jerky or stuttering.[5]
  - Unresponsive UI: User interface elements that are slow to respond to user interactions.
  - Poor user experience: An overall feeling of sluggishness and unresponsiveness.[6]
- Mobile devices, with their limited processing power and screen refresh rates, are particularly susceptible to rendering performance issues.[7]

Network Performance:

- Network operations are a common source of performance bottlenecks in many applications.[8]
- Issues related to network performance can include:
    - Slow network connections: Limited bandwidth or high latency can significantly impact loading times.[9]
    - Large data transfers: Sending or receiving large amounts of data can be slow and consume excessive bandwidth.[10]
    - Inefficient API calls: Poorly designed or implemented APIs can result in slow response times or unnecessary data transfer.[11]
- Network performance is often variable and unpredictable, making it crucial to optimize network operations.[12]

Native Module Overhead:

- If your cross-platform application uses native modules to access platform-specific features, the communication between JavaScript and native code can introduce some overhead.[13]
- Each time you call a native function from JavaScript, there's a cost associated with bridging between the two environments.[14]
- Excessive or inefficient use of native modules can negatively impact performance, especially if these calls are frequent or involve large data transfers.[15]

Platform-Specific Limitations:

- It's important to remember that different platforms have different hardware and software limitations.[16]
- An application that performs well on a high-end desktop computer might struggle on a low-end mobile device or an older web browser.
- Factors like CPU speed, memory availability, graphics processing power, and operating system capabilities can all influence performance.

Techniques for Identifying Performance Bottlenecks

To effectively address performance issues, you need to be able to identify their root causes.

Here are some essential techniques:

Profiling Tools:

- Profiling tools are invaluable for analyzing the performance of your application and pinpointing areas where it's spending the most time or resources.[17]
- These tools provide detailed information about:
  - CPU usage: Which parts of your code are consuming the most processing power.
  - Memory usage: How your application is allocating and using memory, including potential memory leaks.
  - Function call times: How long it takes to execute different functions.
  - Rendering performance: Frame rates, draw calls, and other rendering metrics.

JavaScript Profiling:

- Web browsers provide built-in developer tools that include powerful JavaScript profilers.[18] These allow you to record and analyze JavaScript execution, identify performance bottlenecks in your code, and optimize critical sections.
- Node.js also offers profiling capabilities that can be used to analyze CPU usage and memory consumption in your server-side JavaScript code.[19]

Mobile Profiling:

- Mobile development platforms offer platform-specific profiling tools.[20]
- For iOS, Xcode Instruments is a powerful suite of tools that allows you to profile CPU usage, memory allocation, energy consumption, and other performance metrics.[21]
- For Android, Android Profiler, integrated into Android Studio, provides similar capabilities for analyzing CPU, memory, and network usage.[22]

Performance Monitoring:

- Profiling provides a snapshot of performance at a specific point in time.[23] Performance monitoring, on the other hand, involves tracking performance over time in real-world scenarios.[24]
- This involves:
  - Collecting metrics: Gather data about how your application performs in different situations.

- Analyzing metrics: Identify trends, patterns, and anomalies in the collected data.
- Key metrics to monitor include:
  - Frame rate: The number of frames rendered per second, which is a crucial indicator of UI smoothness.[25]
  - Memory usage: The amount of memory your application is consuming, which can indicate potential memory leaks or inefficient memory management.[26]
  - CPU usage: The percentage of processing power your application is using, which can reveal computationally intensive operations.[27]
  - Network request times: The time it takes for your application to send and receive data over the network, which can highlight network bottlenecks.
- Monitoring can be done using:
  - Built-in platform tools: Some platforms provide tools for monitoring application performance.
  - Third-party performance monitoring services: These services provide comprehensive monitoring capabilities, including error tracking, crash reporting, and performance analysis.[28]

User Feedback and Observation:

- Don't underestimate the value of user feedback in identifying performance issues.
- Users are often the first to notice problems like:
  - Slow loading times: Applications that take a long time to start or load content.
  - UI lag: User interface elements that are slow to respond to interactions.

- Unresponsive behavior: Applications that freeze or become unresponsive.
- Pay close attention to user reviews, bug reports, and support requests. This feedback can provide valuable insights into real-world performance bottlenecks that might not be apparent during development.

By combining these techniques, you can develop a comprehensive approach to identifying performance bottlenecks in your cross-platform applications. This will enable you to focus your optimization efforts on the areas that will have the greatest impact on user experience.

8.2 Optimizing Node.js for Different Environments

Okay, let's focus on optimizing Node.js, a crucial aspect of cross-platform development, especially when your application relies on a Node.js backend. Node.js applications can be deployed in a variety of environments, and optimizing them for each environment is essential for achieving optimal performance, scalability, and reliability.

When we talk about "different environments," we're referring to the various contexts in which your Node.js application might run.

This includes:

- Development Environment: This is where you write and test your code on your local machine.
- Staging Environment: This is a pre-production environment used for testing and quality assurance before releasing to production.
- Production Environment: This is the live environment where your application is accessed by end-users.

Each of these environments has different requirements and characteristics. For example, a development environment might prioritize ease of debugging, while a production environment prioritizes performance and stability.

Here are some key optimization techniques to consider when deploying Node.js applications in different environments:

Code Optimization:

- Efficient Code Writing:
  - Writing efficient Node.js code is the foundation of performance optimization.
  - This involves:
    - Avoiding unnecessary computations.
    - Minimizing memory allocations.
    - Using efficient algorithms and data structures.
    - Optimizing loops and function calls.
  - For example, instead of iterating through a large array multiple times, try to perform all necessary operations in a single loop.
- Asynchronous Operations:
  - Node.js is designed to be asynchronous, and leveraging asynchronous operations is crucial for preventing blocking the event loop.
  - Blocking the event loop can lead to unresponsive applications and performance degradation.
  - Use asynchronous functions (async/await) and non-blocking I/O operations whenever possible.
- Minimizing Dependencies:
  - External dependencies can add overhead to your application.
  - Carefully evaluate the need for each dependency and avoid including unnecessary libraries.
  - Consider using built-in Node.js modules when appropriate.

Memory Management:

- Memory Leaks:
    - Memory leaks can cause your Node.js application to consume excessive memory over time, eventually leading to slowdowns or crashes.
    - Use memory profiling tools to identify and fix memory leaks.
    - Be mindful of variable scope, closures, and event listeners, as these are common sources of memory leaks.
- Garbage Collection:
    - Understand how Node.js's garbage collector works and how to optimize memory usage to assist the garbage collector.
    - Avoid creating unnecessary objects and reuse existing objects when possible.
- Buffers:
    - When working with binary data, use Buffers efficiently.
    - Allocate Buffers appropriately and avoid unnecessary Buffer copies.

Network Optimization:

- Efficient API Design:
    - If your Node.js application serves as a backend API, design your API endpoints to be efficient.
    - Minimize the amount of data transferred in each request and response.
    - Use appropriate HTTP methods and status codes.
    - Implement caching to reduce the load on your server.
- Compression:
    - Compress data before sending it over the network to reduce bandwidth usage and improve loading times.
    - Use compression algorithms like gzip or Brotli.

- Connection Pooling:
  - If your Node.js application interacts with a database, use connection pooling to reduce the overhead of establishing new database connections.

Process Management and Scalability:

- Process Managers:
  - Use process managers like PM2 or Forever to manage and monitor your Node.js processes.
  - These tools can help with:
    - Process restarts in case of crashes.
    - Load balancing across multiple CPU cores.
    - Performance monitoring and logging.
- Clustering:
  - Node.js can utilize all available CPU cores using the cluster module.
  - Clustering allows you to scale your application horizontally to handle increased traffic.
- Load Balancing:
  - For high-traffic applications, use load balancing to distribute the load across multiple Node.js instances.
  - This can improve performance and reliability.

Environment-Specific Configuration:

- Configuration Management:
  - Configure your Node.js application for the specific environment it's running in.
  - Use environment variables or configuration files to manage environment-specific settings.
  - Examples of environment-specific settings include:
    - Database connection strings
    - API keys
    - Logging levels

- Caching settings
- Development vs. Production:
  - Configure your application differently for development and production.
  - In development, you might prioritize ease of debugging and logging.
  - In production, you prioritize performance, stability, and security.

A Practical Exercise

Let's do a practical exercise to demonstrate Node.js optimization:

1. Create a Simple Node.js API:
   - Create a basic Node.js API that performs a computationally intensive task (e.g., sorting a large array, performing complex calculations).
2. Benchmark the API:
   - Use a tool like ab (Apache Benchmark) or autocannon to benchmark the API's performance.
   - Measure the response time and the number of requests per second.
3. Optimize the API:
   - Apply some of the optimization techniques discussed above, such as:
     - Code optimization
     - Asynchronous operations
     - Caching (if applicable)
4. Benchmark Again:
   - Benchmark the API again after optimization and compare the results.

By understanding and applying these optimization techniques, you can ensure that your Node.js applications perform optimally in different environments, contributing to a better user experience and a more efficient system.

8.3 Profiling and Debugging Techniques

Okay, let's talk about profiling and debugging techniques. These are essential skills for any developer, and they are particularly crucial when working on cross-platform applications where you might encounter performance issues or bugs that are specific to certain environments.

Profiling and debugging are the processes of:

- Profiling: Analyzing the performance of your application to identify bottlenecks and areas for optimization.
- Debugging: Identifying and resolving errors or unexpected behavior in your code.

Both are indispensable for ensuring that your applications are performant, stable, and reliable.

Profiling Techniques

Profiling involves using tools and techniques to measure and analyze the performance of your application. This helps you understand how your application is using resources like CPU, memory, and network.

Here are some key profiling techniques:

JavaScript Profiling:

- If your cross-platform application involves JavaScript (which it likely does), JavaScript profiling is crucial.

Browser Developer Tools:

- Modern web browsers provide powerful developer tools that include JavaScript profilers.
- These profilers allow you to:
    - Record JavaScript execution.
    - Analyze CPU usage.
    - Identify functions that are taking a long time to execute.
    - Visualize the call stack.
- This information helps you pinpoint performance bottlenecks in your JavaScript code.

Node.js Profiling:

- Node.js also offers profiling capabilities.
- You can use Node.js profiling tools to:
    - Analyze CPU usage in your Node.js applications.
    - Measure memory consumption.
    - Identify performance bottlenecks in your server-side JavaScript code.

Memory Profiling:

- Memory profiling helps you understand how your application is using memory.
- This is crucial for:

- Identifying memory leaks: Situations where your application is holding onto memory that it no longer needs, leading to increased memory consumption over time.
- Optimizing memory usage: Finding ways to reduce the amount of memory your application uses, which can improve performance and prevent crashes.

Browser Developer Tools:

- Browser developer tools often include memory profiling features that allow you to:
  - Take snapshots of memory usage.
  - Track memory allocations over time.
  - Identify objects that are consuming a lot of memory.

Node.js Profiling Tools:

- Node.js profiling tools can also be used to analyze memory usage in Node.js applications.

Network Profiling:

- Network profiling helps you analyze how your application is communicating with servers or other network resources.
- This is important for:

- Identifying network bottlenecks: Slow or inefficient network requests can significantly impact application performance.
- Optimizing API calls: Analyzing the size and efficiency of your API requests and responses.
- Reducing data transfer: Finding ways to minimize the amount of data transferred over the network.

Browser Developer Tools:

- Browser developer tools provide network tabs that allow you to:
  - Inspect network requests.
  - Analyze request and response headers.
  - Measure the time it takes for requests to complete.

Platform-Specific Profiling Tools:

- When developing for mobile platforms, you should also utilize platform-specific profiling tools.

iOS: Xcode Instruments:

- Xcode Instruments is a powerful suite of performance analysis tools for iOS development.
- It allows you to profile:
  - CPU usage
  - Memory allocation

- o Energy consumption
- o Graphics performance
- o And much more

Android: Android Profiler:

- Android Profiler, integrated into Android Studio, provides similar capabilities for analyzing the performance of your Android applications.
- It allows you to profile:
    - o CPU usage
    - o Memory usage
    - o Network activity
    - o Battery consumption

Debugging Techniques

Debugging involves identifying and resolving errors or unexpected behavior in your code.

Here are some key debugging techniques:

Console Logging:

- console.log() is a basic but essential debugging tool.
- Use it to print values of variables, function calls, and other information to the console to understand the flow of your code and identify potential issues.

Breakpoints:

- Debuggers allow you to set breakpoints in your code, which pause execution at specific points.
- This allows you to:
    - Inspect variables
    - Step through your code line by line
    - Understand the state of your application at a particular moment.

Debuggers:

Browser Developer Tools:

- Browser developer tools include powerful JavaScript debuggers that allow you to set breakpoints, inspect variables, and step through your code.

Node.js Debuggers:

- Node.js also provides debuggers that allow you to debug your server-side JavaScript code.
- You can use Node.js debuggers from your IDE (e.g., VS Code) or from the command line.

Error Handling:

- Implement robust error handling in your code to catch and handle unexpected errors.
- Use try...catch blocks to handle exceptions.
- Provide informative error messages to help with debugging.

Testing:

- Thorough testing is crucial for preventing and detecting bugs.
- Write unit tests, integration tests, and end-to-end tests to verify that your code is working correctly.

A Practical Exercise

Let's do a practical exercise to get you familiar with profiling and debugging:

1. Create a Simple Application:
   - Create a simple web application or a basic Node.js application.
2. Introduce a Performance Bottleneck:
   - Intentionally introduce a performance bottleneck into your application.
   - For example:
     - Inefficient JavaScript code (e.g., a slow loop).
     - A slow network request.
3. Profile Your Application:
   - Use the profiling tools available in your browser developer tools or Node.js to analyze the performance of your application.
   - Identify the performance bottleneck you introduced.

4. **Debug Your Application:**
    - Introduce a bug into your application.
    - Use the debugging tools available in your browser developer tools or Node.js to identify and fix the bug.

By practicing these profiling and debugging techniques, you'll become more adept at identifying and resolving performance issues and bugs in your cross-platform applications, leading to more robust and efficient software.

Chapter 9: Testing Cross-Platform Applications

In this chapter, we'll focus on the different types of testing that are crucial for cross-platform development. We'll cover strategies for writing unit tests, integration tests, and end-to-end tests to ensure that your applications function correctly and consistently across various environments.

9.1 Writing Unit Tests for Node.js Modules

Okay, let's explore in depth the crucial practice of writing unit tests for Node.js modules. This is a fundamental aspect of software development that gains even greater significance when you're building cross-platform applications that heavily rely on Node.js for various functionalities.

What is Unit Testing?

- Unit testing is a method of software testing that focuses on verifying the behavior of individual, isolated parts of your code. The goal is to ensure that each of these parts functions correctly and predictably.
- In the context of Node.js, a "unit" commonly refers to:
  - A function: This is a self-contained block of code designed to perform a specific task. It takes some input, processes it, and produces an output. Unit testing ensures this process works as expected.
  - A method: A function associated with an object or a class. Methods are functions that operate on the data within an object. Unit tests for methods verify that they modify or retrieve data correctly.
  - A small module: A module in Node.js is a self-contained piece of code that exports functionalities to be used elsewhere. Unit tests for

modules verify that these exported functionalities work as intended.

- The key principle here is *isolation*. You aim to test each unit independently, without relying on other parts of your code. This allows you to pinpoint the source of errors more easily.

Why Unit Test Node.js Modules?

- Unit testing provides several compelling benefits, especially when developing cross-platform applications that use Node.js:
  - Ensuring Code Correctness:
    - Unit tests serve as a form of documentation and verification. They provide concrete evidence that your Node.js modules produce the correct output for a given set of inputs.
    - This is paramount for building reliable applications. You want to be confident that your code behaves as expected, especially when it's being used across different platforms.
  - Promoting Code Maintainability:
    - Well-written unit tests make it far easier to refactor and modify your code without inadvertently introducing bugs.
    - When you change the internal implementation of a module, you can run the existing unit tests to quickly verify that you haven't broken any previously working functionality.
    - This is crucial for long-term project health. It allows you to evolve your codebase with confidence.
  - Facilitating Code Reusability:
    - A Node.js module with comprehensive unit tests is much more trustworthy. You can be

more confident in its reliability and correctness.

- This makes the module more suitable for reuse in different parts of your application or even across different projects.
- In cross-platform development, where code sharing between web, mobile, and desktop components is often a key efficiency strategy, this reusability is highly valuable.

Popular Testing Frameworks for Node.js

- Node.js boasts a rich ecosystem of testing frameworks. Here are some of the most popular and effective choices:

Jest:

- Jest is a feature-rich and widely used framework, particularly popular in projects using React.
- It's known for its:
    - Ease of setup and use.
    - Speed of execution.
    - Built-in mocking capabilities, which allow you to simulate the behavior of dependencies.
    - Powerful assertion library for verifying expected outcomes.
    - Excellent code coverage reporting, which helps you understand how much of your code is being tested.

Mocha:

- Mocha is a flexible and adaptable testing framework.
- It provides a core testing structure but allows you to choose your preferred assertion library (e.g., Chai) and mocking library (e.g., Sinon).
- This flexibility makes it suitable for various testing styles.

Jasmine:

- Jasmine is another popular framework, often used for behavior-driven development (BDD).
- It offers a clean and readable syntax for writing tests, making them easy to understand and maintain.

A Practical Example: Unit Testing a Utility Module

- Let's illustrate unit testing with a practical example. Imagine you've created a Node.js module that provides utility functions for working with strings:

JavaScript

```
// string-utils.js

function capitalize(str) {

  if (!str) return '';
```

```javascript
  return str.charAt(0).toUpperCase() +
str.slice(1);

}

function trimWhitespace(str) {

  if (!str) return '';

  return str.trim();

}

module.exports = {

  capitalize,

  trimWhitespace,

};
```

Here's how you might write unit tests for this module using Jest:

JavaScript

```javascript
// string-utils.test.js
```

```javascript
const stringUtils =
require('./string-utils');

describe('stringUtils', () => {

  describe('capitalize', () => {

    it('should capitalize the first letter
of a string', () => {


expect(stringUtils.capitalize('hello')).toBe
('Hello');

    });

    it('should return an empty string if
input is empty', () => {


expect(stringUtils.capitalize('')).toBe('');

    });

  });

  describe('trimWhitespace', () => {

    it('should remove leading and trailing
whitespace', () => {
```

```
    expect(stringUtils.trimWhitespace('  hello
')).toBe('hello');


    });


    it('should return an empty string if
input is empty', () => {


    expect(stringUtils.trimWhitespace('')).toBe(
'');


    });


    });


});
```

In this example:

- ○ describe blocks are used to group related tests, providing structure and readability.
- ○ it blocks define individual test cases, each testing a specific aspect of a function's behavior.
- ○ expect assertions are used to verify the expected output of the functions.

Best Practices for Unit Testing Node.js Modules

- To write effective and maintainable unit tests for your Node.js modules, consider these best practices:

Test Every Unit:

- Aim to write unit tests for every function, method, and module in your Node.js code.
- This ensures that all parts of your code are covered by tests, minimizing the risk of undetected bugs.

Isolate Units:

- Ensure that your unit tests test each unit in isolation.
- Use mocking or stubbing to replace any dependencies that the unit might have.
- Mocking allows you to simulate the behavior of external modules or services, so you can focus solely on testing the unit itself.

Write Clear and Readable Tests:

- Your tests should be easy to understand and maintain.
- Use descriptive names for your test cases and organize your tests logically to improve readability.

Run Tests Frequently:

- Run your unit tests frequently, especially after making changes to your code.

- This helps you catch bugs early and prevent regressions, ensuring that new code doesn't break existing functionality.

Aim for High Code Coverage:

- Code coverage measures the percentage of your code that is covered by unit tests.
- Aim for high code coverage to ensure that most of your code is tested.
- However, remember that code coverage is just one metric, and it's important to write meaningful tests that cover different scenarios and edge cases, not just aim for a high percentage.

A Practical Exercise

- To solidify your understanding of unit testing, try this practical exercise:

Create a Node.js Module:

- Create a simple Node.js module with a few functions (e.g., a module for date formatting, a module for data validation).

Choose a Testing Framework:

- Select a testing framework (Jest, Mocha, or Jasmine) to use for your tests.

Write Unit Tests:

- Write unit tests for your module, covering various scenarios, input values, and edge cases.
- For example, if you have a date formatting function, test different date formats, invalid dates, and boundary conditions.

Run Your Tests:

- Run your tests using the chosen testing framework.
- Verify that all your tests pass and that your module behaves as expected.

By diligently writing unit tests for your Node.js modules, you'll build a more robust, reliable, and maintainable codebase, which is essential for successful cross-platform development.

9.2 Integration Testing Across Platforms

Okay, let's explore integration testing in the context of cross-platform development. This is a crucial phase of testing that goes beyond individual units and focuses on how different parts of your application work together.

What is Integration Testing?

- Integration testing is a type of software testing that verifies the interaction and communication between different units or components of your application.

- While unit testing focuses on isolated units, integration testing examines how these units function when combined. It's about testing the "interfaces" between these units.
- This could involve testing:
    - The interaction between different modules in your codebase.
    - The communication between different layers of your application (e.g., the presentation layer and the data access layer).
    - The integration with external systems, such as APIs or databases.

Why is Integration Testing Important for Cross-Platform Development?

- Integration testing becomes particularly important in cross-platform development due to the inherent complexity of these projects.
- Here's why:

Verifying Interoperability: Cross-platform applications often involve various technologies and components that need to work together seamlessly.

This might include:

- Front-end code written in JavaScript.
- Back-end APIs built with Node.js.
- Native components or modules for platform-specific features.
- Integration testing helps ensure that these components are compatible and function correctly in conjunction, regardless of the target platform.

Identifying Interface Issues: Integration testing can reveal problems with the interfaces between different units or components.

These problems might include:

- Incorrect data exchange: Units passing the wrong type of data or in the wrong format.
- Mismatched data types: Units expecting different data types, leading to errors.
- Errors in communication protocols: Issues with how units communicate, such as incorrect headers or message formats.

Ensuring System-Level Functionality: Integration testing verifies that the application's core functionality works as expected when different parts of the system are combined. This is crucial for ensuring that the application meets its overall requirements and delivers the intended user experience on all target platforms.

Integration Testing Strategies for Cross-Platform Applications

- When designing your integration testing strategy for cross-platform applications, consider these approaches:

Testing API Integrations: If your cross-platform application relies on backend APIs (which is very common), integration testing should focus on verifying the communication and interaction between the front-end (e.g., web or mobile app) and the API.

This includes:

- Testing API endpoints: Ensuring that the API endpoints return the correct data, handle different types of requests (e.g., GET, POST, PUT, DELETE), and respond with the appropriate HTTP status codes.
- Testing data exchange formats: Verifying that data is correctly formatted and parsed between the front-end and the API. This often involves ensuring that data is sent and received in JSON format as expected.
- Testing authentication and authorization: Ensuring that users are correctly authenticated (e.g., logged in) and authorized to access specific resources or perform certain actions.

Testing Framework Interactions: If your cross-platform application uses frameworks like Electron (for desktop) or React Native (for mobile), integration testing should verify how your application interacts with these frameworks.

This might include:

- Testing the communication between the main process and renderer processes in Electron applications.
- Testing the integration of native components or modules in React Native applications, ensuring they function correctly within the app's structure.

Testing Platform-Specific Components: If your cross-platform application uses native modules or platform-specific components to access features on certain platforms, integration testing should verify how these components interact with the rest of the application. This ensures that platform-specific code is correctly integrated and doesn't introduce any conflicts or issues with the shared codebase.

A Practical Example: Integration Testing a React Native App with a Node.js API

- Let's consider a practical example of integration testing a React Native application that fetches data from a Node.js API:

API Testing:

- Use tools like Jest or Supertest (a library for testing HTTP APIs) to test the Node.js API endpoints.
- Verify that they return the correct data, handle different request types, and respond with appropriate HTTP status codes.

React Native Integration Testing:

- Use React Native testing libraries (e.g., React Native Testing Library) to test the React Native components that interact with the API.
- Verify that these components correctly fetch data from the API, display it to the user, and handle different states (e.g., loading, error, success).

End-to-End Integration Testing (Optional):

- Use testing frameworks like Detox (for React Native) or Appium (a general-purpose mobile testing framework) to test the entire flow, from user interaction in the React Native app to data retrieval from the Node.js API.
- This would involve simulating user actions and verifying that the entire process works as expected.

Best Practices for Integration Testing

- To perform effective integration testing, consider these best practices:

Define Clear Integration Points:

- Identify the key integration points in your application. These are the specific points where different units or components interact and exchange data.
- Clearly defining these points will help you focus your testing efforts.

Start with Small Integrations:

- Begin by testing small, simple integrations and gradually increase the scope of your tests.
- This allows you to identify and fix issues early before they become more complex.

Use Mocking and Stubs:

- Use mocking or stubbing techniques to isolate the components you're testing and simulate the behavior of dependencies.
- This allows you to focus on testing the integration itself without being affected by the behavior of other units.

Test Different Scenarios:

- Test various scenarios, including normal cases (expected behavior), edge cases (unusual input or conditions), and error conditions (unexpected input or failures).
- This ensures that your integration handles different situations gracefully.

Automate Integration Tests:

- Automate your integration tests as much as possible so they can be run frequently, such as in a Continuous Integration/Continuous Delivery (CI/CD) pipeline.
- This ensures that integrations are tested regularly and that new code changes don't break existing integrations.

A Practical Exercise

- To solidify your understanding of integration testing, try this practical exercise:

Create a Simple Cross-Platform Application:

- Create a basic cross-platform application with a Node.js backend and a front-end (e.g., a React Native app or a simple web app).

Identify Integration Points:

- Identify the key integration points between the front-end and the backend, such as data fetching, user authentication, or form submission.

Choose a Testing Framework/Library:

- Choose a testing framework or library suitable for your front-end (e.g., React Testing Library for React Native) and a tool for testing your API (e.g., Supertest for Node.js).

Write Integration Tests:

- Write integration tests to verify the communication and data exchange between the front-end and the backend for the identified integration points.

Run Your Tests:

- Run your tests and verify that the integration works as expected, ensuring that data is exchanged correctly and that the different components function together.

By implementing effective integration testing strategies, you can ensure that the different parts of your cross-platform applications work together correctly, leading to a more robust, reliable, and user-friendly experience across all platforms.

9.3 End-to-End Testing with Emulators and Simulators

Okay, let's explore end-to-end (E2E) testing in the context of cross-platform applications. This is a critical stage of testing that focuses on verifying the entire application flow and user experience.

What is End-to-End Testing?

End-to-end (E2E) testing is a software testing methodology that verifies the complete flow of an application from start to finish.[1] It simulates real user scenarios and validates the application's functionality as a whole, including all its components and dependencies.[2]

Unlike unit testing, which tests individual units in isolation, and integration testing, which tests the interaction between units, E2E testing takes a holistic approach.[3] It aims to ensure that the application functions correctly from the user's perspective, mimicking how a user would interact with the application in a real-world setting.[4]

E2E testing typically involves:

- Simulating user actions, such as clicking buttons, filling out forms, or navigating through different screens.[5]
- Verifying that the application responds correctly to these actions.
- Validating that data is processed and displayed as expected.
- Ensuring that all components of the application, including the front-end, back-end, and any external systems, work together seamlessly.

Why is End-to-End Testing Important for Cross-Platform Development?

End-to-end testing becomes particularly important in cross-platform development due to the inherent complexity of these projects.[6]

Here's why:

Verifying User Flows Across Platforms:

- Cross-platform applications often have complex user flows that span across different components and potentially different platforms.
- For example, a user might start a process on a web browser, continue it on a mobile app, and complete it on a desktop application.
- E2E testing helps ensure that these flows work correctly and consistently for users, regardless of the platform they are using.

Identifying System-Level Issues:

- E2E testing can uncover system-level issues that might not be apparent during unit or integration testing.[7]
- This includes problems such as:
    - Data persistence issues: Problems with how data is stored and retrieved.[8]
    - Network communication errors: Issues with how the application communicates with backend APIs or other services.
    - Interactions between different parts of the application: Problems that arise when different components are combined in a real-world scenario.

Ensuring a Consistent User Experience:

- One of the key goals of cross-platform development is to provide users with a consistent and predictable experience across different platforms.
- E2E testing plays a crucial role in achieving this goal by verifying that the application functions and behaves in a similar way for users on all target platforms.[9]
- This is essential for user satisfaction and adoption, as users expect applications to be intuitive and reliable, regardless of the device or operating system they are using.[10]

End-to-End Testing Strategies for Cross-Platform Applications

- When designing your E2E testing strategy for cross-platform applications, consider these approaches:

Testing User Interactions:

- E2E testing should simulate real user interactions with the application as closely as possible.[11]
- This might involve:
    - Testing user login and registration flows.
    - Testing navigation between different screens or sections of the application.
    - Testing data input, such as filling out forms or entering text.
    - Testing the interaction with different UI elements, such as buttons, links, and menus.[12]

Testing Data Flow:

- E2E testing should verify the flow of data through the application's various components.[13]
- This includes:
    - Testing data persistence, ensuring that data is correctly stored and retrieved from databases or local storage.[14]
    - Testing data synchronization, verifying that data is correctly synchronized between different components or devices.
    - Testing data exchange with backend APIs, ensuring that data is sent and received correctly.

Testing Platform-Specific Functionality:

- If your cross-platform application uses native modules or platform-specific functionality, E2E testing should verify that these features work correctly in the context of the overall application flow.
- For example, if you're using a native module for accessing the device's camera, your E2E tests should include scenarios that involve using the camera functionality.

End-to-End Testing with Emulators and Simulators

Emulators and simulators are software tools that allow you to run and test your application on virtual devices.[15] They are incredibly valuable for cross-platform development because they provide a way to test your application on different platforms and devices without needing to have access to a large collection of physical devices.[16]

Here's the difference between them:

Emulators

Emulators simulate the hardware and software of a real device.[17] They provide a more accurate representation of the device's behavior but can be slower and more resource-intensive to run. Emulators are often used for testing Android applications.[18]

Simulators

Simulators provide a lighter-weight and faster way to test your application. They simulate the operating system but might not accurately represent the device's hardware. Simulators are often used for testing iOS applications.[19]

Using Emulators and Simulators for E2E Testing:

- You can use emulators and simulators to run your E2E tests on a wide range of platforms and devices.[20] This allows you to:
    - Verify that your application functions correctly on different operating systems (e.g., iOS, Android).
    - Test your application on different device models (e.g., different iPhone models, different Android phone models).
    - Simulate different network conditions or other environmental factors that might affect your application's behavior.[21]
- E2E testing frameworks like Appium and Detox are specifically designed to automate your E2E tests on emulators and simulators.[22] These frameworks provide APIs for interacting with UI elements, simulating user actions, and verifying application behavior.[23]

Best Practices for End-to-End Testing

- To perform effective end-to-end testing, consider these best practices:

Define Clear Test Scenarios:

- Carefully identify the key user flows and scenarios that need to be tested.
- These scenarios should represent typical user interactions with your application and cover the most important functionalities.

Write Robust and Reliable Tests:

- Your E2E tests should be robust and reliable. They should be able to run consistently and produce predictable results.
- Avoid flaky tests that fail intermittently or depend on specific timing or network conditions.[24]

Use a Testing Framework:

- Utilize a dedicated E2E testing framework like Appium or Detox to automate your E2E tests.[25]
- These frameworks provide powerful features for interacting with UI elements, simulating user actions, and verifying application behavior.[26]

Test on Real Devices When Possible:

- While emulators and simulators are valuable tools, it's also important to test your application on real devices whenever possible.[27]
- Real devices provide a more accurate representation of the user experience and can reveal issues that might not be apparent in emulators or simulators.[28]

Automate E2E Tests:

- Automate your E2E tests so they can be run frequently, such as in a Continuous Integration/Continuous Delivery (CI/CD) pipeline.[29]
- This ensures that E2E tests are executed regularly and that new code changes don't introduce regressions in the application's overall functionality.

A Practical Exercise

- To solidify your understanding of end-to-end testing, try this practical exercise:

Create a Simple Cross-Platform Application:

- Create a basic cross-platform application (e.g., a simple to-do list app, a basic e-commerce app).

Choose an End-to-End Testing Framework:

- Select an E2E testing framework suitable for your project (e.g., Appium or Detox).

Set up an Emulator or Simulator:

- Set up an emulator or simulator for your target platform (e.g., Android emulator, iOS simulator).

Write End-to-End Tests:

- Write E2E tests to verify the key user flows of your application, such as:
    - User login and registration.
    - Adding, editing, and deleting data.
    - Navigating between different screens or sections of the application.

Run Your End-to-End Tests:

- Run your E2E tests on the emulator or simulator.
- Verify that the application functions correctly and that the user flows work as expected.

By implementing effective end-to-end testing strategies and utilizing emulators and simulators, you can ensure that your cross-platform applications provide a consistent, reliable, and user-friendly experience across different platforms and devices.

Chapter 10: Debugging and Troubleshooting

In this chapter, we'll equip you with the knowledge and skills to effectively identify, diagnose, and resolve issues that arise during the development and deployment of your cross-platform applications. We'll cover debugging platform-specific problems, using debugging tools and techniques, and identifying common pitfalls and their solutions.

10.1 Debugging Platform-Specific Issues

Okay, let's explore in detail the challenges and strategies involved in debugging platform-specific issues in cross-platform development. This is a crucial skill, as you'll often encounter problems that manifest differently or only appear on particular operating systems or devices.

When developing for multiple platforms, you're essentially working with a codebase that interacts with diverse environments. Each of these environments has its own unique characteristics, APIs, behaviors, and limitations. This diversity inevitably leads to situations where your application behaves inconsistently.

The Nature of Platform-Specific Issues

Here are some common categories of platform-specific issues that developers frequently encounter:

UI Rendering Differences:

- Even when using cross-platform UI frameworks, achieving pixel-perfect consistency across all platforms can be a significant challenge.
- You might find variations in:

- o Layout: Elements might be positioned or sized differently on different screens.
  - o Styling: CSS styles might be interpreted or applied differently by different rendering engines.
  - o Component Behavior: UI components might have subtle differences in their behavior or interactions.
- For example, a button might look and feel slightly different on iOS compared to Android, or a web page might render differently in various browsers.

Native Module Issues:

- If your cross-platform application relies on native modules to access platform-specific features, you're introducing a layer of complexity that can lead to platform-specific problems.
- These issues can include:
  - o Communication problems: Errors in the way JavaScript code interacts with the native code.
  - o Native module functionality: The native module might not function correctly or might have limitations on certain platforms.
  - o Dependency conflicts: Conflicts between the native libraries used by your module and other libraries on the system.

Device-Specific Behavior:

- In some cases, issues might only occur on specific devices or device models. This is particularly common in mobile development.

- Factors that can contribute to device-specific behavior include:
  - Hardware limitations: Differences in CPU speed, memory, or graphics processing power.
  - Operating system versions: Variations in the behavior of different OS versions.
  - Device-specific configurations: Settings or configurations that are unique to certain devices.

Operating System Quirks:

- Each operating system has its own set of quirks, idiosyncrasies, and design choices. These can lead to unexpected behavior in your application.
- Examples include:
  - File system access: Differences in how files are stored and accessed.
  - Networking: Variations in network protocols or behavior.
  - Memory management: Different ways in which the operating system manages memory.
  - Background tasks: How the operating system handles tasks running in the background.

Strategies for Debugging Platform-Specific Issues

Effectively debugging platform-specific issues requires a combination of knowledge, tools, and techniques.

Here are some key strategies:

Leveraging Platform-Specific Developer Tools:

- The first and often most crucial step is to utilize the developer tools provided by each platform. These tools are designed to help you inspect, analyze, and debug applications in their respective environments.

Web Browsers:

- Modern web browsers come equipped with powerful developer tools. These tools are invaluable for debugging issues in web-based cross-platform applications.
- Key features include:
    - HTML and CSS inspection: Allows you to examine the structure and styling of your web pages.
    - JavaScript debugger: Enables you to set breakpoints, step through code, inspect variables, and analyze JavaScript execution.
    - Network monitoring: Allows you to inspect network requests and responses, analyze performance, and identify network-related issues.

Mobile Development Tools:

- Mobile development platforms also provide platform-specific debugging tools.

Xcode (iOS):

- Xcode, Apple's integrated development environment (IDE), includes a comprehensive debugger.
- Key features include:
    - Debugging native code (Objective-C or Swift).
    - Inspecting variables and memory.
    - Stepping through code execution.
    - Using Instruments, a suite of performance analysis tools.

Android Studio:

- Android Studio, Google's IDE for Android development, provides a robust debugger.
- Key features include:
    - Debugging native code (Kotlin or Java).
    - Inspecting variables and memory.
    - Stepping through code execution.
    - Using Android Profiler, a tool for analyzing CPU, memory, and network usage.

Logging and Error Reporting:

- Implementing comprehensive logging within your application is essential for tracking its behavior and identifying potential issues.
- Include informative error messages that provide context and details about any errors that occur.
- For production environments, consider using error reporting tools or services that can automatically collect and analyze errors, providing valuable insights into issues that users are experiencing.

Testing on Real Devices:

- While emulators and simulators are useful for initial testing, it's crucial to test your application on real devices, especially when debugging platform-specific issues.
- Real devices provide a more accurate representation of the user experience and can reveal issues that might not be apparent in virtual environments.

Isolating the Issue:

- When you encounter a platform-specific issue, try to isolate it as much as possible. This involves:
    - Simplifying your code: Reduce the complexity of your code to pinpoint the source of the problem.
    - Removing unnecessary components: Temporarily remove parts of your application to see if the issue persists.

- Creating a minimal reproducible example: Try to create a small, self-contained piece of code that demonstrates the issue.
- Isolating the issue will make it significantly easier to diagnose and fix.

By employing these strategies and utilizing the appropriate tools, you can effectively debug platform-specific issues in your cross-platform applications, leading to more robust and reliable software.

10.2 Using Debugging Tools and Techniques

Okay, let's explore the essential topic of using debugging tools and techniques. Effective debugging is a cornerstone of software development, and mastering these tools and techniques is crucial for efficiently identifying and resolving issues in your cross-platform applications.

Debugging is the process of finding and fixing errors or bugs in your code. These errors can manifest in various ways, from unexpected behavior to application crashes. Debugging tools and techniques provide the means to investigate these issues, understand their causes, and implement solutions.

Here are some essential debugging tools and techniques that every cross-platform developer should be familiar with:

Breakpoints:

- Breakpoints are markers that you set in your code to intentionally pause the execution of the program at a specific point.
- This allows you to:

- Inspect the values of variables at that point in time.
- Examine the state of your application.
- Step through the code line by line to understand the program's flow.

Most debuggers provide features for:

- Setting breakpoints: Placing these markers in your code.
- Stepping over: Executing the next line of code without entering a function call.
- Stepping into: Entering a function call to debug its execution.
- Stepping out: Continuing execution until the current function returns.
- Continuing execution: Resuming normal execution after a breakpoint is hit.

Inspectors:

- Debuggers also provide inspectors or watch windows that allow you to examine the values of variables, objects, and data structures.
- This is crucial for understanding the data flow within your application and identifying any unexpected values or states.
- Inspectors typically allow you to:
  - View the current values of variables.
  - Expand objects to see their properties and values.
  - Evaluate expressions to see the result of calculations.
  - Watch variables to track their changes over time.

Console Logging:

- console.log() is a basic but incredibly useful debugging tool, especially for JavaScript.
- You can use it to print:
    - The values of variables at different points in your code.
    - Messages to indicate the execution flow of your program.
    - Information about function calls and their arguments.
- This helps you understand the sequence of events in your code and identify where problems might be occurring.
- While simple, console.log() is a powerful tool for initial investigation and quick debugging.

Network Monitoring:

- Debugging tools often include network monitoring capabilities, which are essential for applications that communicate with external APIs or services.
- These tools allow you to:
    - Inspect network requests and responses: See the data being sent and received.
    - Analyze request headers and bodies: Examine the structure and content of network messages.
    - Measure the time it takes for requests to complete: Identify network bottlenecks or slow API responses.

This is invaluable for debugging issues related to:

- API integration.
- Data transfer.
- Network connectivity.

Debugging Native Code:

- When working with cross-platform applications that use native modules, you might need to debug the native code itself.
- This requires using platform-specific debugging tools:

Xcode (iOS):

- Xcode provides a powerful debugger for Objective-C or Swift code.
- It allows you to set breakpoints, inspect variables, step through code execution, and analyze memory usage in your native iOS code.

Android Studio:

- Android Studio includes a robust debugger for Kotlin or Java code.

- It offers features similar to Xcode's debugger, enabling you to debug your native Android code effectively.

A Practical Exercise

To gain hands-on experience with debugging tools and techniques, I recommend the following exercise:

1. Create a Simple Application:
   - Create a simple web application or a basic Node.js application.
2. Introduce a Bug:
   - Intentionally introduce a bug into your application. This could be a logical error, a syntax error, or any other type of error that causes unexpected behavior.
3. Use Debugging Tools:
   - Use the debugging tools available for your chosen platform or environment (e.g., browser developer tools, Node.js debugger) to:
     - Set breakpoints in your code.
     - Inspect the values of variables.
     - Step through your code line by line.
4. Identify and Fix the Bug:
   - Use the information you gather from the debugging tools to identify the root cause of the bug.
   - Implement a solution to fix the bug.
5. Verify the Fix:
   - Run your application again to verify that the bug is resolved and that your application now behaves as expected.

By practicing these debugging techniques, you'll become more proficient at identifying and resolving errors in your cross-platform applications, leading to more robust and reliable software.

10.3 Common Cross-Platform Pitfalls and Solutions

Okay, let's explore some of the common pitfalls that developers often encounter when working on cross-platform applications, along with practical solutions to help you avoid or overcome them.

Cross-platform development offers many benefits, but it also presents unique challenges. Being aware of these potential pitfalls will help you make informed decisions and build more robust and successful applications.

Here are some of the common cross-platform pitfalls:

UI Inconsistencies:

- Even when using cross-platform UI frameworks, achieving a truly consistent user interface across different platforms can be difficult.
- This is because each platform has its own set of UI conventions, design guidelines, and rendering engines.

You might encounter variations in:

- Layout: Elements might be positioned or sized differently on different screens.
- Styling: CSS styles might be interpreted or applied differently, leading to visual discrepancies.

- Component Behavior: UI components might have subtle differences in their behavior or interactions, affecting the user experience.

Solution:

- Thorough Testing on All Target Platforms: Rigorous testing on a variety of devices and operating systems is essential to identify and address UI inconsistencies.
- Platform-Specific Styling or Components (When Necessary): In some cases, you might need to use platform-specific styling or components to ensure a native look and feel. This can involve using conditional logic in your code or using platform-specific UI libraries.
- Adherence to Platform-Specific UI Guidelines: Carefully adhere to the design guidelines of each target platform (e.g., Apple's Human Interface Guidelines for iOS, Google's Material Design for Android). This helps to create a more familiar and intuitive experience for users.

Performance Issues:

- Performance is a critical consideration in any application, but it becomes even more challenging in cross-platform development.
- Performance can vary significantly across different platforms and devices.
- Factors that can contribute to performance issues include:

- JavaScript overhead: JavaScript execution can be slower than native code, especially in complex applications.
- Rendering performance: Rendering UI elements and animations can be more demanding on some platforms than others.
- Device limitations: Mobile devices often have limited processing power and memory compared to desktop computers.

Solution:

- Optimize Your Code for Performance: Write efficient code, minimize unnecessary computations, and use appropriate data structures and algorithms.
- Use Asynchronous Operations: Leverage asynchronous operations to prevent blocking the main thread and ensure responsiveness.
- Minimize Data Transfer: Optimize your network requests and data transfer to reduce bandwidth usage and improve loading times.
- Profile Your Application on Different Platforms: Use platform-specific profiling tools to identify performance bottlenecks and optimize critical sections of your code.
- Consider Platform-Specific Performance Optimizations: In some cases, you might need to implement platform-specific optimizations to achieve optimal performance. This could involve using native modules or platform-specific APIs.

Platform-Specific Bugs:

- In addition to performance variations, you might encounter bugs that only occur on specific platforms or devices.
- These bugs can be caused by:
    - Differences in the underlying operating systems.
    - Variations in hardware implementations.
    - Issues with the cross-platform framework itself.

Solution:

- Test Your Application on a Wide Range of Devices and Platforms: Thorough testing on a variety of devices and operating systems is crucial for identifying platform-specific bugs.
- Implement Comprehensive Logging and Error Reporting: Use logging to track application behavior and capture error messages. This can help you pinpoint the source of platform-specific problems.
- Utilize Platform-Specific Debugging Tools: Use the debugging tools provided by each platform (e.g., Xcode for iOS, Android Studio for Android) to diagnose and fix platform-specific bugs.

Native Module Integration Challenges:

- Integrating native modules to access platform-specific features can introduce complexity and potential issues.
- These challenges can include:

○ Communication issues between JavaScript and native code.
○ Compatibility problems with native module functionality on certain platforms.
○ Dependency conflicts with native libraries.

Solution:

- Use Native Modules Only When Necessary: Avoid using native modules unless they are absolutely required for accessing platform-specific functionality.
- Design Clear and Consistent Interfaces for Native Modules: Create well-defined APIs for your native modules to ensure smooth communication with JavaScript code.
- Test Your Native Modules Thoroughly on Each Platform: Rigorous testing is essential to ensure that native modules function correctly and don't introduce platform-specific issues.
- Manage Platform-Specific Dependencies Carefully: Use appropriate dependency management tools (e.g., CocoaPods for iOS, Gradle for Android) and carefully manage version compatibility.

Testing Complexity:

- Testing cross-platform applications can be more challenging than testing single-platform applications due to the need to test on multiple environments.

Solution:

- Use Automated Testing Tools and Frameworks: Employ automated testing tools and frameworks to streamline the testing process and ensure consistent test execution across different platforms.
- Prioritize End-to-End Testing: Focus on end-to-end testing to verify the overall application flow and user experience on each platform.
- Use Emulators and Simulators for Efficient Testing: Utilize emulators and simulators to test your application on a wide range of virtual devices, which can be more efficient than testing on physical devices.
- Test on Real Devices When Possible: Complement emulator/simulator testing with testing on real devices to ensure that your application performs correctly in real-world conditions.

By being aware of these common cross-platform pitfalls and implementing the suggested solutions, you can develop more robust, reliable, and user-friendly applications that provide a consistent and positive experience across different platforms.

Chapter 11: Best Practices and Security

In this chapter, we'll explore best practices for building cross-platform applications, with a strong emphasis on security considerations. We'll also discuss strategies for maintaining and scaling your projects, and we'll examine real-world case studies to illustrate successful cross-platform development.

11.1 Security Considerations for Cross-Platform Apps

Okay, let's talk in detail about security considerations for cross-platform applications. Security is a paramount concern in any software development project, but it takes on even greater importance when you're building applications that target multiple platforms. The reason is simple: you're essentially increasing the potential attack surface and introducing new vulnerabilities that might be specific to certain environments.

When you develop for a single platform, you can tailor your security measures to the specific characteristics of that platform. However, in cross-platform development, you need to consider the security implications of each platform you're targeting and ensure that your application is robust and protected against a wide range of threats.

Here's a breakdown of key security considerations for cross-platform apps:

Input Validation:

- Input validation is a fundamental security practice that should be implemented rigorously in any application, but it's especially crucial in cross-platform development.

What it is: Input validation involves carefully checking and sanitizing any data that enters your application from external sources.

This includes:

- User input from forms or other UI elements.
- Data received from APIs or external services.
- Data read from files or databases.

The goal is to ensure that the data is in the expected format, range, and type, and that it doesn't contain any malicious or unexpected content.

Why it's important:

- Input validation helps prevent common security vulnerabilities that can be exploited to compromise your application or system. These vulnerabilities include:
  - SQL Injection: This occurs when malicious code is injected into database queries, potentially allowing attackers to access, modify, or delete data in your database.
  - Cross-Site Scripting (XSS): This occurs when malicious scripts are injected into web pages viewed by other users. These scripts can be used to steal user credentials, hijack user sessions, or deface websites.
  - Command Injection: This occurs when malicious commands are injected into system commands,

potentially allowing attackers to execute arbitrary code on the server.

- Proper input validation also helps to ensure that your application handles data correctly and doesn't crash or behave unexpectedly due to invalid input.

Best Practices:

- Whitelist Allowed Characters: Instead of trying to block every possible malicious character, focus on defining a set of allowed characters for each input field. This is a more secure approach.
- Sanitize Input: Remove or escape any potentially harmful characters from the input before using it. This might involve encoding special characters or removing potentially dangerous code.
- Validate Data Types and Formats: Ensure that the input matches the expected data type and format. For example, if you're expecting a number, verify that the input is indeed a number. If you're expecting an email address, validate that it has a valid email format.

Authentication and Authorization:

Authentication and authorization are critical security mechanisms that are essential for protecting sensitive data and controlling access to your application's features.

Authentication: This is the process of verifying the identity of a user. It answers the question, "Who is this user?"

Common authentication methods include:

- Username and password authentication.
- Multi-factor authentication (MFA).
- Biometric authentication (e.g., fingerprint or facial recognition).

Authorization: This is the process of determining what a user is allowed to do within the application. It answers the question, "What can this user access or do?"

Best Practices:

- Use Strong Password Hashing Algorithms: Never store passwords in plain text. Instead, use strong password hashing algorithms to store a one-way representation of the password. This makes it much harder for attackers to obtain user passwords if your database is compromised.
- Implement Secure Authentication Protocols: Consider using well-established and secure authentication protocols such as OAuth 2.0 or other modern authentication methods. These protocols provide robust security features and are designed to protect against common authentication attacks.

Apply the Principle of Least Privilege: Grant users only the necessary permissions to perform their tasks. Avoid giving users excessive privileges, as this increases the potential damage if their account is compromised.

Data Security:

- Protecting sensitive data is paramount in any application, but it's particularly important in cross-platform development, where data might be stored or transmitted across different environments.

Data in Transit:

- Data in transit refers to data that is being transmitted between your application and servers or other systems.
- Use HTTPS (Hypertext Transfer Protocol Secure) to encrypt communication between your application and servers. HTTPS uses SSL/TLS encryption to protect data from being intercepted or read by unauthorized parties.
- Avoid sending sensitive data over unencrypted connections. This includes data transmitted over HTTP or other insecure protocols.

Data at Rest:

- Data at rest refers to data that is stored locally on the device or on the server.

- Encrypt sensitive data that is stored locally on the device. This might include using platform-specific encryption mechanisms or libraries.
- Use secure storage mechanisms provided by the operating system or framework. For example, use secure storage APIs provided by iOS or Android for storing sensitive data on mobile devices.

Cross-Site Scripting (XSS) Prevention:

- Cross-site scripting (XSS) attacks can be particularly dangerous in web-based or hybrid cross-platform applications, where web technologies are used to render the user interface.

What it is: XSS occurs when malicious scripts are injected into web pages viewed by other users.

These scripts can be used to:

- Steal user credentials or session cookies.
- Hijack user sessions.
- Deface websites or display malicious content.

How to prevent it:

Sanitize User Input: Carefully escape or encode any user-provided data that is displayed on the page. This prevents malicious scripts from being executed in the user's browser.

Use a Framework's Built-in XSS Protection: Many web frameworks provide built-in mechanisms to prevent XSS attacks. These mechanisms often involve automatically escaping or encoding potentially dangerous characters.

Security in Native Module Integration:

- If your cross-platform application uses native modules to access platform-specific features, you need to be particularly careful about security.

What to consider:

Vulnerable Dependencies: Ensure that the native libraries or SDKs you use in your native modules are up-to-date and free from known vulnerabilities. Regularly check for security advisories and update your dependencies as needed.

Code Injection: Be cautious about how you pass data from JavaScript to native code, as this can be a potential attack vector.

Carefully validate any data received from JavaScript in your native code to prevent malicious input from being processed.

Secure Communication: If your native module communicates with external systems or services, ensure that the communication is secure. Use encryption and authentication mechanisms to protect data in transit.

Regular Security Updates:

- Security threats are constantly evolving, so it's crucial to keep your application and its dependencies up-to-date.

What to do:

- Regularly Update Your Cross-Platform Framework, Libraries, and Native Modules: This ensures that you have the latest security patches and are protected against known vulnerabilities.
- Monitor Security Advisories: Stay informed about security vulnerabilities in the frameworks, libraries, and dependencies you use. Subscribe to security advisories and patch vulnerabilities promptly.

By carefully considering these security aspects and implementing robust security measures, you can build cross-platform applications that are more resilient to attacks and protect user data effectively.

11.2 Maintaining and Scaling Cross-Platform Projects

Okay, let's discuss the critical aspects of maintaining and scaling cross-platform projects. As your application grows in complexity and user base, it's essential to have strategies in place to ensure its long-term health and ability to handle increasing demands.

Maintaining and scaling cross-platform projects presents unique challenges due to the need to support multiple platforms and potentially large codebases.

Here's a breakdown of key strategies:

Modular Architecture:

- A modular architecture is a cornerstone of maintainability and scalability in any software project, but it's particularly vital in cross-platform development.

What it is: A modular architecture involves breaking down your application into smaller, self-contained units called modules. Each module should have a specific responsibility and a well-defined interface.

Benefits:

Easier to understand and modify: Modules are self-contained, making them easier to grasp and work with. This reduces the cognitive load on developers and simplifies code changes.

Improved code reuse: Modules can be shared across different parts of the application or even across different projects, promoting efficiency and reducing redundancy.

Simplified testing: Modules can be tested in isolation, making it easier to verify their functionality and identify bugs.

Scalability: Modules can be scaled independently, allowing you to optimize performance and resource usage for specific parts of the application.

Example: In a cross-platform application, you might have modules for:

- User authentication.
- Data management.
- UI components.
- Network communication.

Code Sharing Strategies:

- Maximizing code reuse across different platforms is a key strategy for reducing development and maintenance effort in cross-platform projects.

Here are some effective techniques:

Shared Libraries:

- Create reusable libraries (often in Node.js or similar) that contain common logic that can be used by all platforms.
- These libraries can encapsulate:

Monorepos:

- Use a monorepo (a single repository containing multiple related projects) to manage the code for your web, mobile, and desktop applications, along with any shared libraries.
- Tools like Lerna or Yarn Workspaces can help you manage dependencies and build processes within a monorepo.
- Monorepos facilitate code sharing and collaboration by keeping all related code in a single place.

Automated Testing:

- Automated testing is crucial for ensuring the quality and stability of your application as it evolves. This is even more important in cross-platform development, where you need to verify functionality across different environments.
- Here are the key types of tests:

Unit Tests:

- These tests verify the functionality of individual units of code (e.g., functions, methods, modules) in isolation.
- They ensure that each unit behaves as expected and that changes to one unit don't break other units.

Integration Tests:

- These tests verify how different units or components of your application work together.
- They ensure that the interactions between these units are correct and that data is exchanged properly.

End-to-End Tests:

- These tests verify the entire application flow from start to finish, simulating real user scenarios.
- They ensure that all components of the application, including the front-end, back-end, and external systems, work together seamlessly.

Continuous Integration/Continuous Delivery (CI/CD):

- CI/CD is a set of practices that automate the build, test, and deployment process. It's essential for streamlining your development workflow and ensuring efficient releases.

Benefits:

- Faster and more reliable releases: CI/CD automates the release process, reducing the risk of errors and speeding up deployment.
- Improved code quality: Automated testing in CI/CD pipelines helps to catch bugs early in the development process, preventing them from reaching production.
- Simplified collaboration: CI/CD provides a centralized and automated way to manage the development process, improving collaboration among developers, testers, and operations teams.

Performance Monitoring:

- Monitoring the performance of your application in production is crucial for identifying and addressing potential bottlenecks.
- Key metrics to monitor include:
    - CPU usage: Track how much processing power your application is consuming.
    - Memory usage: Monitor memory consumption to identify potential leaks or inefficiencies.
    - Network request times: Measure how long it takes for network requests to complete.

- o Error rates: Track the frequency of errors to identify areas of instability.

Scalability Considerations:

- Design your application with scalability in mind to ensure it can handle increasing user loads and data volumes.
- Techniques to consider include:
    - o Load balancing: Distributing traffic across multiple servers to prevent overload.
    - o Caching: Storing frequently accessed data in memory to reduce[1] database load and improve response times.
    - o Asynchronous operations: Using asynchronous operations to prevent blocking the main thread and ensure responsiveness.

By implementing these strategies, you can build cross-platform projects that are not only functional but also maintainable, scalable, and resilient in the long run.

11.3 Real-World Case Studies

Okay, let's explore some real-world case studies to illustrate the practical application and success of cross-platform development. Examining how companies have leveraged these technologies can provide valuable insights and inspiration.

It's important to note that the definition of "cross-platform" can vary. In some cases, it might refer to sharing code between web and mobile, while in others, it might involve building desktop applications that run on multiple operating systems.[1]

Here are some examples of applications and companies that have successfully employed cross-platform development strategies:

Applications Built with Electron:

- Electron, a framework that allows you to build desktop applications with web technologies (HTML, CSS, and JavaScript), has been used to create a number of popular applications.[2]

Slack: The popular communication platform uses Electron to build its desktop applications for Windows, macOS, and Linux.[3] This allows Slack to maintain a consistent user experience across different operating systems while leveraging web development skills.[4]

Discord: Another popular communication platform, especially among gamers, also relies on Electron for its desktop applications.[5] Electron's cross-platform capabilities enable Discord to reach a wide user base without requiring separate development efforts for each OS.[6]

VS Code (Visual Studio Code): Microsoft's popular code editor is built with Electron.[7] This allows developers to use a single codebase to create a powerful and versatile editor that runs on various desktop platforms.

Key Takeaways from Electron Case Studies:

- Electron demonstrates the feasibility of building complex and feature-rich desktop applications using web technologies.[8]
- It allows companies to leverage web development skills to create cross-platform desktop applications.[9]
- It can significantly reduce development time and effort compared to building native applications for each operating system.[10]

Applications Built with React Native:

- React Native, a framework that enables building native mobile applications using JavaScript and React, has also been adopted by many companies.[11]

Facebook: Facebook itself uses React Native for parts of its mobile applications.[12] This allows them to share code between their iOS and Android apps, improving development efficiency.

Instagram: Another Facebook-owned platform, Instagram, also utilizes React Native for certain features.[13] This highlights how React Native can be used to build performant and engaging mobile experiences.

Airbnb: Although Airbnb famously moved away from React Native for large portions of its app, they did use it for a significant period.

Their experience provides valuable lessons in the trade-offs of React Native development for complex, large-scale applications. They ultimately found that the "native" nature of the underlying implementations offered performance and UX benefits as they scaled.

Key Takeaways from React Native Case Studies:

- React Native is a viable option for building cross-platform mobile applications with JavaScript.[14]
- It can lead to significant code sharing between iOS and Android, reducing development effort.
- However, projects should carefully consider the trade-offs and potential limitations, especially for large, complex applications or projects needing very tight native performance.

Important Note:

- These case studies provide insights into the successful use of cross-platform technologies.
- However, it's essential to remember that the best approach for cross-platform development depends on the specific requirements of each project.

Factors to consider include:

- Project complexity
- Performance requirements

- Budget and timeline constraints
- Development team expertise

By examining these real-world examples, you can gain a better understanding of the strengths and limitations of different cross-platform technologies and how they can be used to build successful applications.

Chapter 12: Emerging Trends and Technologies

In this chapter, we'll look ahead at the technologies and trends that are poised to influence the future of cross-platform application development. We'll discuss WebAssembly, future directions in Node.js, and the broader evolution of multi-platform apps.

12.1 WebAssembly and Cross-Platform Potential

Okay, let's explore WebAssembly (Wasm) and its potential impact on cross-platform development. This is a technology that's generating a lot of excitement, and for good reason! It has the potential to fundamentally change how we build and deploy applications, particularly in web-based contexts, and that has significant implications for cross-platform development.

What is WebAssembly?

To understand WebAssembly's potential, we need to first grasp what it is. At its core, WebAssembly is a binary instruction format for a stack-based virtual machine.[1]

Let's break that down:

Binary instruction format: This means that WebAssembly code is not human-readable like JavaScript. It's a low-level format that's designed to be executed directly by a computer.[2]

Stack-based virtual machine: WebAssembly code runs in a virtual machine (VM) that uses a stack data structure to perform operations.[3] This is a common way that low-level code is executed.

In essence, WebAssembly is a way to run code in web browsers that's very different from how JavaScript works.[4] JavaScript is a high-level, interpreted language.[5] This means that it's designed to be relatively easy for humans to read and write, but it's executed by the browser's JavaScript engine, which interprets the code at runtime.

WebAssembly, on the other hand, is a low-level, assembly-like language.[6] This means that it's much closer to the machine code that a computer's processor understands. WebAssembly code is typically compiled from other languages, such as C++, Rust, or C#, before it's run in the browser.[7]

The key difference is that WebAssembly code can be executed much faster than JavaScript code.[8] Because it's already in a low-level format, the browser doesn't have to spend time interpreting it.

How Does WebAssembly Relate to Cross-Platform Development?

WebAssembly's speed and capabilities have significant implications for cross-platform development, particularly in the web context.[9]

Here's how:

Performance-Critical Applications: WebAssembly is especially valuable for applications that require high performance and where JavaScript's limitations might become a bottleneck.[10] This includes applications like:

Games: Complex 3D games or games with heavy physics calculations can benefit greatly from WebAssembly's speed.[11]

3D Graphics: Web applications that need to render complex 3D scenes or perform advanced graphics operations can leverage WebAssembly for better performance.[12]

Scientific Simulations: Applications that perform complex scientific calculations or simulations can use WebAssembly to run those calculations efficiently in the browser.[13]

Complex Calculations: Any application that involves heavy mathematical computations or data processing can benefit from WebAssembly's speed.[14]

The traditional approach would be to try and optimize JavaScript code to achieve the desired performance.

With WebAssembly, you have a powerful alternative:

You could write the performance-critical parts of your application in a language like C++, Rust, or C#.

Then, you compile that code to WebAssembly to run in the browser.

This allows you to leverage the performance of native-like code while still using web technologies (HTML, CSS, JavaScript) for the user interface and other parts of the application.[15]

Code Reuse: WebAssembly can potentially facilitate code reuse across different platforms, which is a major goal in cross-platform development.[16]

The idea is that you could potentially compile the same core code to WebAssembly to run in a web browser and to native code for other platforms (e.g., iOS, Android, desktop).[17]

This could significantly reduce the amount of platform-specific code you need to write and maintain.

o

Example

To make this more concrete, consider an example of developing a game:

- You want your game to run in a web browser (for accessibility) and also as a native application on desktop and mobile platforms.
- You could write the game's core logic (e.g., game engine, physics, AI) in C++, a language known for its performance.[18]
- Then:

- You could compile the C++ code to WebAssembly to run the game in a web browser.[19]
- You could also compile the C++ code to native code (e.g., for Windows, macOS, iOS, Android) to create native versions of the game.

This allows you to share a significant portion of the game's code between different platforms, reducing development effort and improving performance.

Current State and Future Trends

- It's important to note that WebAssembly is a relatively new technology, but it's rapidly evolving and gaining traction.[20]
- Browser support for WebAssembly is growing steadily, and it's already being used in a variety of applications, from games and graphics-intensive tools to productivity applications.[21]
- Looking ahead, we can expect to see WebAssembly become even more prevalent in web development. As the technology matures and tooling improves, it will likely play an increasingly important role in cross-platform development, offering a powerful way to achieve native-like performance in web-based applications and potentially facilitate greater code sharing across different platforms.

12.2 Future Directions in Node.js Cross-Platform Development

Okay, let's explore the future directions of Node.js and its evolving role in cross-platform development. Node.js has already established itself as a powerful tool in web development, but its influence is expanding, and it's important to consider where it might be headed in the context of building applications for multiple platforms.

Node.js, primarily known for its server-side JavaScript capabilities, is demonstrating increasing versatility. While its core strength will likely remain in backend development, its influence in other areas is worth exploring.

Here are some key trends and future directions to consider:

Node.js for More Than Backend:

Node.js's runtime environment, which allows JavaScript execution outside the browser, has opened doors for its use in various applications beyond traditional server-side development.

Desktop Development:

Electron, a framework built on Node.js, has become a prominent tool for building cross-platform desktop applications.

This trend is likely to continue, with Node.js playing a significant role in empowering developers to create desktop applications for Windows, macOS, and Linux using web technologies.

We can expect to see further improvements and refinements in Electron and related technologies, making Node.js an even more compelling option for desktop development.

Tooling:

Node.js has become a dominant force in the development of build tools, command-line interfaces (CLIs), and other essential development tools.

This trend is expected to persist, with Node.js continuing to be a key technology for creating tools that streamline and enhance the development process for cross-platform applications.

Performance Enhancements:

The Node.js runtime is constantly being optimized for performance. The Node.js community and the Node.js project itself are dedicated to making Node.js faster and more efficient.

We can expect to see ongoing improvements in:

JavaScript Execution Speed: V8, the JavaScript engine that powers Node.js, is continually being refined to execute JavaScript code more quickly.

Asynchronous Operations: Node.js's asynchronous nature is a core strength, and further optimizations in this area will improve the performance of I/O-bound operations.

Memory Management: Efforts to improve memory management within Node.js will lead to more efficient and scalable applications.

These performance enhancements will directly benefit cross-platform applications that rely on Node.js, making them more responsive and capable.

Improved WebAssembly Integration:

WebAssembly (Wasm) is a technology that enables running code written in other languages in web browsers at near-native speed. It's poised to have a significant impact on web development and cross-platform development.

As WebAssembly matures and becomes more widely adopted, we can anticipate tighter integration between Node.js and WebAssembly.

This could open up exciting possibilities for Node.js applications to leverage WebAssembly for performance-critical tasks, such as:

- High-performance computing within Node.js.
- Running computationally intensive tasks more efficiently.
- Potentially sharing code between Node.js and the browser in new ways.

Enhanced Cross-Platform APIs:

- o To simplify cross-platform development, we might see the development of new Node.js APIs or modules that provide a more consistent and unified way to access platform-specific features.
- o This could reduce the need for developers to rely on native modules or platform-specific code, making cross-platform development more streamlined and less complex.
- o For example, we could see standardized APIs for accessing common device features or operating system services, abstracting away the platform differences.

Node.js is not only a powerful server-side technology but also a versatile tool that continues to evolve and adapt to the changing landscape of software development. Its future directions hold exciting possibilities for cross-platform development, making it an increasingly important player in the creation of applications for multiple platforms..

12.3 The Evolving Landscape of Multi-Platform Apps

Okay, let's explore the evolving landscape of multi-platform applications. The way we build and use software is constantly changing, and it's essential to understand the trends that are shaping the future of developing for multiple platforms.

The term "multi-platform" can encompass various scenarios, including web, mobile, and desktop applications. The key idea is building software that can reach users on different devices and operating systems.

Here are some key trends and factors that are driving the evolution of multi-platform apps:

Increased Demand for Cross-Platform Solutions:

The need to reach users on a wide range of platforms will continue to be a major driver for the development of cross-platform solutions.

Businesses and developers want to:

Maximize their reach: They want their applications to be accessible to as many potential users as possible, regardless of the devices or operating systems they use.

Minimize development costs: Building separate applications for each platform can be expensive and time-consuming. Cross-platform development aims to reduce the effort and resources required.

This demand is fueled by the increasing diversity of devices and platforms, including:

- Smartphones and tablets (iOS and Android).
- Desktop computers (Windows, macOS, Linux).
- Web browsers (various browsers on different platforms).

Maturity of Cross-Platform Frameworks:

Cross-platform frameworks have been evolving and maturing significantly over the years. This makes them more viable and attractive options for building multi-platform apps.

Frameworks like:

React Native: A popular framework for building native mobile apps with JavaScript and React.

Flutter: A UI toolkit developed by Google for building natively compiled applications for mobile, web, and desktop from a single codebase.[1]

These frameworks are offering:

Improved performance: They are getting closer to native performance in many cases.

More robust features: They are providing a wider range of functionalities and capabilities.

Better developer experiences: They are becoming easier to use and more efficient for developers.

The Rise of Progressive Web Apps (PWAs):

Progressive Web Apps (PWAs) are a significant trend that's blurring the lines between traditional web applications and native mobile apps.

What are PWAs?

PWAs are web applications that are designed to provide a native-like experience to users.

They leverage modern web technologies to offer features that were previously only available to native apps.

Key features of PWAs:

Offline access: PWAs can work even when the user is offline or has a poor internet connection.

Push notifications: PWAs can send push notifications to users, keeping them engaged.

Installation: PWAs can be installed on users' devices, appearing as native apps.

Improved performance: PWAs can be optimized for fast loading and smooth performance.

Impact on Multi-Platform Development:

PWAs are becoming an increasingly important part of the multi-platform landscape.

They offer a way to deliver a rich application experience across different platforms using web technologies.

PWAs can be a viable alternative to native apps in some cases, especially for applications that don't require access to highly specific native features.

Focus on User Experience:

The importance of providing a high-quality user experience across all platforms is constantly growing.

Users expect applications to be:

Performant: Fast, responsive, and smooth.

Accessible: Usable by people with disabilities.

Intuitive: Easy to use and understand.

Visually appealing: Well-designed and consistent with platform-specific design guidelines.

This emphasis on user experience is driving developers to:

Pay close attention to performance optimization.

Design with accessibility in mind.

Consider the native look and feel of each platform.

In summary, the landscape of multi-platform apps is dynamic and evolving.

The key trends are:

- Increased demand for solutions that reach users across various platforms.
- The increasing maturity and capability of cross-platform frameworks.
- The rise of Progressive Web Apps (PWAs) as a powerful alternative.
- A strong emphasis on delivering a high-quality user experience on all platforms.

Understanding these trends is crucial for developers who want to build successful and future-proof applications in the multi-platform era.

Conclusion

This book has aimed to provide a comprehensive exploration of mastering Node.js for cross-platform web development. We've journeyed through the fundamentals of Node.js, explored advanced techniques, and considered the evolving landscape of multi-platform applications. By now, you should have a solid foundation for building robust, scalable, and efficient applications that reach users across various platforms.

We began by establishing the core need for cross-platform solutions in today's diverse technological environment. We examined different cross-platform approaches, highlighting the strategic role Node.js plays in enabling these solutions. We then revisited essential Node.js concepts, emphasizing asynchronous JavaScript, the event loop, module systems, and server building – all critical for cross-platform development.

The book then progressed to advanced techniques, focusing on architecting applications for cross-platform compatibility. We discussed designing platform-agnostic APIs, creating reusable Node.js modules, and implementing abstraction layers to handle platform differences effectively. We also explored framework integrations, specifically how Node.js works with Electron for desktop applications and React Native/NativeScript for mobile development, along with strategies for code sharing to maximize efficiency.

A crucial aspect of this exploration was the emphasis on building and deploying multi-platform applications. We covered build automation, setting up CI/CD pipelines, and leveraging Docker for efficient and consistent deployment across different environments. We also addressed the critical aspects of performance optimization, including identifying bottlenecks, optimizing Node.js, and utilizing profiling and debugging tools.

Testing was given due attention, covering unit testing for Node.js modules, integration testing across platforms, and end-to-end testing with emulators and simulators. These testing strategies are essential for ensuring the quality, reliability, and consistency of your applications across diverse platforms.

Throughout this book, we've also stressed the importance of security, discussing key security considerations for cross-platform applications, from input validation to data security, authentication, and XSS prevention. We also explored best practices for maintaining and scaling cross-platform projects, recognizing the need for modular architecture, code sharing, and performance monitoring.

Finally, we looked towards the future, examining emerging trends and technologies such as WebAssembly and the evolving landscape of multi-platform apps. This forward-looking perspective equips you to adapt to the ever-changing world of software development.

By combining theoretical knowledge with practical examples and exercises, this book has sought to empower you to build cross-platform applications with confidence. The techniques and strategies discussed here are designed to help you navigate the complexities of multi-platform development and create applications that are both effective and user-friendly.

The journey of mastering Node.js for cross-platform development is an ongoing one. The technologies and best practices will continue to evolve. However, the principles and techniques outlined in this book provide a strong foundation for your continued growth and success in this dynamic field.

www.ingramcontent.com/pod-product-compliance
Lightning Source LLC
LaVergne TN
LVHW081521050326
832903LV00025B/1577